"Prayer ought to be enjoyable! After all, Scripture tells us, 'In [God's] presence is the fullness of joy' (Psalm 16:11), and the essence of prayer is to engage with God's presence. Matthew Lilley makes this reality come wonderfully alive in his excellent and timely book *Enjoying Prayer*. Read it! Live it! Enjoy it! Then, take that joy into your times of prayer and watch God multiply it daily!"

Dr. Dick Eastman
Past President of Every Home for Christ (1988-2022)
President of America's National Prayer Committee

"Matthew Lilley has done us all a great service by setting forth an excellent treatment of prayer. He grounds prayer squarely where it should be in the relational nature of God—as Father, Son, and Holy Spirit—with love of and union with God as prayer's ultimate purpose and goal. His insight into what makes enjoyable prayer is matched with a refreshing vulnerability that both the person beginning in prayer and the mature believer will be tremendously enriched. This work is crucial for the discipleship of the next generation of believers."

Allen Hood, MDiv, Asbury Theological Seminary
Director of Excellencies of Christ Ministries

"In this new book by Matthew Lilley, a seed of hope is planted within the longing heart of those who have struggled with prayer. Learning to find joy and soul satisfaction in the secret place requires more than good intentions, it demands practical means. *Enjoying Prayer* is filled with revelation from a life dedicated to prayer as well as practical insights of how to create an atmosphere

in which our spirit soars in fellowship with God. I am grateful for this new work and whole-heartedly endorse it."

Lee Cummings
Senior Leader of Radiant Church and Radiant Network of Churches, Author of *School of the Spirit* and *Give No Rest!*

"Without a doubt, Matthew Lilley gives us the missing ingredient of effective prayer — the joy of the Lord! Jesus is not just a King with power but a passionate Bridegroom full of joy over his bride! This book is packed with practical tips to encounter the God who overflows with joy for his people. Read and ENJOY!"

Dr. Jason Hubbard
Director of International Prayer Connect

"This book title says it all. The latest book from Matthew peels back the complexities that religion has taught us about prayer and helps us rediscover the beauty of prayer and relationship with God. In a moment that church culture is again awakening to prayer as being essential in our practice and liturgy, this book comes at a prophetic time for the Lord's people. I have had the honor of being Matthew's pastor for many years. There is no one better to help us all learn how to enjoy prayer."

Aaron Kennedy
Pastor of Opendoor Church

ENJOYING PRAYER

Knowing God and Transforming the World

Matthew Lilley

©2023 by Matthew Lilley

All rights reserved. No part of this book may be used or reproduced in any manner whatsoever without written permission, except in the case of brief quotations in critical articles and reviews. For more information and permission, write to: admin@inscribepress.com.

Published by Presence Pioneers Media, Farmville, NC
Cover design by Mary Beth Barefoot.
    Contact her at marybethbarefoot@gmail.com.
Edited by Jeffrey Pelton.
Printed in the United States of America.

ISBN 978-1-951611-56-9 (print)
       978-1-951611-57-6 (e-book)

This title is also available as an audiobook.

Unless otherwise indicated, Scripture quotations are from The ESV® Bible (The Holy Bible, English Standard Version®), copyright © 2001 by Crossway, a publishing ministry of Good News Publishers. Used by permission. All rights reserved.

DEDICATION

For my father who is now in heaven with our Father.
Thank you for always encouraging me to write books.

Ronald Earl Lilley
1945-2023

CONTENTS

Introduction / 1

Part One: Foundations for Enjoyable Prayer
    Love: The Purpose of Prayer / 7
    Our Father: The Object of Prayer / 19
    Sonship: Our Identity in Prayer / 31
    First: The Priority of Prayer / 43

Part Two: Keys to Enjoyable Prayer
    Worship: Combining Music and Prayer / 59
    Scripture: The Language of Prayer / 69
    Listening: Hearing God's Voice in Prayer / 81
    Persistence: Staying Faithful in Prayer / 93

Part Three: Transformation Through Enjoyable Prayer
    Intercession: Partnership with God in Prayer / 107
    Tongues & Travail: Spirit-Filled Prayer / 121
    Fasting: Hunger for God Through Prayer / 133

Part Four: The House of Enjoyable Prayer
    Together: The Need for Corporate Prayer / 147
    Unceasing: A Movement of Day & Night Prayer / 157

About the Author / 169
Bibliography / 171
Other works / 173

Introduction

If you took a poll of Christians and asked them to describe their prayer lives, I am guessing the word "enjoyable" would be towards the bottom of the list. And yet, there is an incredible promise in the Bible about enjoying prayer:

> "These I will bring to my holy mountain, and make them joyful in my house of prayer" (Isaiah 56:7).

Here we have the infallible word of God declaring that His people will pray together and like it! It seems like a pipe dream. How do we get from where we are to this promised place of enjoyable prayer? Trying to figure that out is the purpose of this book.

At the time of this writing, I have been in full-time vocational prayer ministry for over fifteen years. You might assume that I always enjoy prayer, that I'm "good" at it or that I've become an expert on the subject. That is far from the truth. While I *have* spent many hours in private and corporate prayer and I *have* spent a lot of time studying what the Bible says about prayer, prayer can still be a struggle for me. Sitting in a room, staring at the ceiling and talking to someone you can't see is still weird sometimes. I still get distracted a lot.

I want to be honest with you upfront. When I talk about enjoying prayer, I am not trying to be idealistic about building a relationship with a God that we cannot see with our eyes. On my best days, I go deep into Scripture with the Holy Spirit in prayer—meditating and dwelling on the truth about who God is and the incredible plans He has outlined in His word. On the worst days, my prayer times are hijacked by thoughts about bills and my kids and if I need to repaint the trim in my house and that interaction I had with a coworker and how I need to eat healthier and... God easily gets lost in the mix. Perhaps you can relate. Or perhaps you struggle to pray at all.

If you're looking for a book from an expert intercessor or "prayer warrior" then you'll need to look elsewhere. In fact, I could probably give you some good suggestions. However, if you're willing to hear from someone who is called to prayer ministry but still struggles with prayer, then I'm here for you.

Because the truth is, I have grown to love prayer. I have had some amazing times interacting with the Lord alone in my private prayer times and in prayer meetings. I've discovered that a real relationship with an invisible God is possible — not only possible, but indescribably *enjoyable*. I've seen God answer my prayers, sometimes in dramatic ways. I've seen prayer that resulted in miraculous physical healing, unexpected financial breakthrough, crime rates dropping, weather patterns being altered and more. Prayer can be powerful and fun! But I also know it can sometimes be awkward and hard. So if you are okay with learning from someone who is consistently inconsistent but hasn't given up yet, then keep reading.

What This Book Is and Is Not

I built everything in this book around the key that released joy in my own prayer life: intimacy with God. If you learn to love God, then you'll love to pray. This book is not a "how to" book, per se. I sprinkle a number of practical tips throughout the chapters, but — because prayer is about relationship with God — the only way to truly learn is to get to know Him.

Rather than being overly practical, I have instead focused on some of the underlying truths about prayer that can help us enter into the intimate relationship God desires for us. Wrong ideas about God, His kingdom, the nature of prayer, the person of the Holy Spirit, and our identity in Christ can become hindrances to enjoyable prayer. Unbiblical mindsets keep us from experiencing the joy of communion with God and partnership with Him in prayer.

Because prayer exists to facilitate our relationship with God, it can hardly be put into a formula. I can share some of what the Bible teaches, some of my own experiences and wisdom I've gleaned from trying to lead others in prayer. But the truth is, relationships are messy, unpredictable and awkward at times. Prayer is too. So this book is not a formula for you to follow. Rather, I hope it acts as a battering ram to break down all the barriers in your life that are keeping you from a joyful, worshipful, intimate, and fruitful relationship with God. That is why there is a lot of Scripture and Bible teaching on these pages. If you open your heart as you read, the truth of God's word will expose lies, encourage your heart, and fill you with faith in God's love and goodness.

An Overview of the Book Chapters

The first four chapters are a section called "Foundations for Enjoyable Prayer." If you misunderstand the purpose of prayer, then you will constantly be frustrated. The first chapter is all about the *why* of prayer. Chapters two and three focus on the *who* of prayer. Jesus taught us to pray to God as our Father, and He encouraged us to relate to Him as sons and daughters. Chapter four is about making prayer a priority in our lives, even when there are setbacks, delays, or a lack of answers.

Chapters five through eight are a section called "Keys to Enjoyable Prayer." Here you will get some of the practical ways to build upon the foundation laid in the previous section. I have found that musical worship, listening to God's voice, praying the Bible, and staying persistent have helped me experience the greatest joy in my prayer life.

The next section, chapters nine through twelve, are called "Transformation Through Enjoyable Prayer." While prayer is first and foremost about knowing and loving God, He also invites you into partnership with Him for His kingdom purposes. This is where your prayers grow from intimacy into intercession. These chapters are the "deeper waters" of the book where we explore intercessory prayer, travailing prayer, praying in tongues, and fasting.

The final section is "The House of Enjoyable Prayer," chapters thirteen and fourteen. Prayer was never meant to be a solo sport. The promise of enjoyable prayer in Isaiah 56:7 specifically mentions praying with others. Our joy is found in the house of prayer — first of all in our local prayer community and secondly as part of the global day & night prayer movement that God is orchestrating around the world.

I hope you enjoy the book, but more importantly, I hope you learn to enjoy prayer.

Part One: Foundations for Enjoyable Prayer

LOVE: THE PURPOSE OF PRAYER

Growing up, I was part of a family that was fully immersed in the evangelical Christian subculture of the 1990s. We went to church multiple times each week. Mom listened to old Integrity praise & worship cassette tapes in our minivan. We took regular trips to our local Christian bookstore. I went to Acquire the Fire,[1] participated in a 30-Hour Famine[2] and listened to loads of CCM albums on my Sony Discman. Some of you have no idea what I am talking about but some of you are having nostalgic flashbacks right now.

In this environment, I was constantly reminded of the importance of prayer. "Read your Bible, pray every day, and you'll grow, grow, grow" is the song we sang in Sunday School. Yet for some reason I never quite understood why prayer was so important. It just seemed like one of those painful things you're supposed to do, like eating your vegetables, doing your homework, or evangelizing people despite being an introvert.

I don't remember where I was when I first noticed the Bible verse that redefined my understanding of Christianity and prayer.

---

1 Acquire the Fire were large Christian youth rallies hosted by Teen Mania Ministries that included concerts, dramas, worship and Bible teachings. https://en.wikipedia.org/wiki/Teen_Mania_Ministries
2 30 Hour Famine is a 30-hour youth lock-in event where teenagers fast for 30 hours to raise money for World Vision and raise awareness of global poverty. https://30hourfamine.worldvision.org/

I had listened to countless sermons about God wanting to give us "eternal life" in heaven. I knew that John 3:16, the most famous Bible verse, said that Jesus died so that we could have "eternal life." I always assumed that eternal life referred to living in heaven forever when we die. That is why Jesus died, right? To get us to heaven? Wasn't that the eternal life He promised to us? For sure, eternity with God in the age to come is a big part of what it means[3]. But then I noticed John 17:3.

Jesus used the phrase "eternal life" quite a lot, but John 17:3 is the place in Scripture where he defines it. In John 17, Jesus the Son is on the earth talking to God the Father in heaven. God is talking to God, and apparently the apostle John is over-hearing and notating the conversation. What an experience! It is the longest prayer of Jesus recorded in the Bible. The entire chapter is full of revelation about the heart of God, the nature of the Trinity, how we should pray, and God's ultimate purposes for His people.

Right at the beginning of his prayer, Jesus drops a bombshell:

> And this is eternal life, that they know you, the only true God, and Jesus Christ whom you have sent. John 17:3

Jesus defined eternal life as *knowing God*. *"For God so loved the world that He sent His only Son that whoever believes in Him will not perish but will...."* Know God. Have eternal life. This redefined my whole understanding of Christianity and the gospel. God didn't just save me so that I could work for Him and help save more people who could also work for Him. He wanted to know me. The issue that drove Christ to the cross was not that God needed evangelists but that your relationship with God was broken. He

---

3   See Matthew 25,46 John 10:28

wants you to know and love Him. That is why Christ came — to give you eternal life, which is a right relationship with Him.

The First and Greatest Commandment

One time Jesus was approached by a lawyer who asked Him about the greatest commandment in the law[4]. As usual, this was an attempt to trap and humiliate Jesus with a seemingly unanswerable question — a play right out of the Pharisees' book. I like to imagine myself in this story. I would provide Jesus with a great comeback. As a lifelong Sunday school attendee, I would have had the perfect answer for him. I can hear my ten-year-old, know-it-all voice right now: "Actually, Mr. Lawyer…. there is no verse in the Bible greater than the others because it is all God's word and it is all important."

Jesus shocks us by answering the lawyer's question. Apparently the incarnate Son of God had a favorite Bible verse. Here's His answer.

> And he said to him, "You shall love the Lord your God with all your heart and with all your soul and with all your mind. This is the great and first commandment. And a second is like it: You shall love your neighbor as yourself. On these two commandments depend all the Law and the Prophets."
> Matthew 22:37-40

My ten-year-old self would have been correct in one sense. All Scripture is God's word and is valuable to us[5]. But certain parts of Scripture seem to have priority over the others in how we understand what's important to the Lord. Jesus says unequivocally that what is most important to God is that we love him and love others. All Scripture is filtered through this truth: God wants people to love Him. This is what He is working towards, cultivating

---

[4] Matthew 22:35-36
[5] 2 Timothy 3:16

and orchestrating right now in you, in me, and throughout the earth. Jesus calls this command to love God the "great" and "first" commandment. Mike Bickle says that God is working to put the "first commandment in first place."[6]

As theologians have attempted to summarize the overall theme of the Bible, many propositions have been put forth. Recently, an Old Testament scholar and a New Testament scholar teamed up to examine the entirety of Scripture for a common thread that holds everything together. Their conclusion was that the "megatheme" of the Bible was *God's relational presence*. Every book of the Bible resonates with the truth that God wants us to be with Him and to know Him.

> "... the cohesive central megatheme of God's relational presence connects all...other themes into the big overarching plot of the biblical story. In our view, most... other major biblical themes are actually 'subplots' (so to speak), each of which is interconnected and related to the megastory of God's relational presence."[7]

The theologians are catching up to what Jesus taught us long ago. We were made for love. We were made for God. Loving Him is the first and greatest commandment. This biblical paradigm shapes our understanding of everything we do as Christians. All of our spiritual disciplines, discipleship, holiness, and missions efforts are about humanity entering into a loving relationship with God.

The Purpose of Prayer is Love

Prayer exists as a means to experience God's relational presence. The purpose of prayer is love. Whether it be prayers of thanksgiving, intercession, praise, repentance, petition or spiritual

---

6   *Growing in Prayer* pg 114
7   *God's Relational Presence*, page 5

warfare, all true prayer will lead to greater love for God and others. The *why* beyond the *what* of prayer is that God is confronting anything that hinders love in His people and cultivating intimate partnership with us as His children and His Son's bride. God wants you to know Him intimately, which includes a loving partnership with Him in His purposes for the earth. He desires you would be one with Him.

Prayer is not just talking *to* God, prayer is talking *with* God. It is not primarily functional but relational. Prayer is the foundation of your love relationship with Him because it is how you communicate with Him. In fact, communication is at the core of any relationship. So prayer is at the core of knowing God. To look at prayer as primarily functional is to miss the point. Yes, prayer can accomplish things. In fact, it can be a weapon for good in the earth when wielded from the lips of God's people. But God does not need your words to carry out His purposes. He can do anything He wants.[8] Yet He chose to create you and involve you in His universe for a reason. If it's not that God needs you, then it must be that He wants you.

My children sometimes ask me why God created the world if he knew people would sin. It is a great question that is not easily answered or understood. The existence of evil is one of the greatest philosophical challenges for humanity. While I can't comprehend the mystery of God's sovereignty and human choice, I do know one thing: forced love is not love. If God had created you as a robot that could not choose to love Him or not, then you could never love him. I cannot imagine a scenario where love exists unless there is also a choice to not love.

It is God's nature to love. The apostle John famously said that God *is* love[9]. I am confident then that God created the universe

---

[8] Our God is in the heavens; he does all that he pleases. Psalm 115:3
[9] 1 John 4:8

to express His love. You exist because you were made to love God, be loved by God and share that love with others. God's eternal plan is to have a family where love abounds in joy, delight and peace forever. The Father will have sons and daughters and the Son will have a bride. God's people will be one with Him forever. This was God's original intent for humanity. And despite mankind's fall into sin and the subsequent corruption of the earth, the Father has made a way through the life, death, resurrection and ascension of Jesus Christ to make all things new again. Love will reign in the end.

The Promise of Enjoyable Prayer

It took me so long to realize that the purpose of prayer was not primarily to get things accomplished. I assure you that God could snap his fingers and do whatever He wanted to do right now. God is not limited. He does not need your help. Nor will He be persuaded by you. Prayer is not about convincing God to accomplish anything. It is not about earning something from God.

I distinctly recall loathing the times when I forced myself to pray as a young man trying to live rightly for Jesus. I would go to God with my list of wants and needs, speak them to the ceiling and move on with my life. It felt weak and pointless. There was no connection with God. I may as well have been sending emails to God with my prayer requests as attachments. Not only was this boring, but it didn't seem to ever work. I never seemed to notice an answer to any of my prayers. I kept trying to get God to give me what I wanted, but He wouldn't budge. Everyone at church talked about how important it was to pray, but I didn't get it. I was obviously missing the purpose of prayer. I was viewing prayer as a means to access God's resources to accomplish my will, rather

LOVE: THE PURPOSE OF PRAYER

than a way to experience intimacy and partnership with God to accomplish His will. I had also missed James 4:3:

> You ask and do not receive, because you ask wrongly, to spend it on your passions.

It was only when I began to discover intimacy with God, primarily through musical worship, that I really began to understand prayer. And then from the overflow of intimacy, I discovered the power and excitement of intercession, where I could agree with God's word and Spirit to see His power released into the earth. Knowing God's heart through intimacy and worship brought joy to my heart, and learning the art of intercession allowed me to see answers to my prayers like never before. That was exciting! It felt like God and I were in sync together. No more throwing up my prayers to the ceiling in hopes that God might accidentally answer me. I learned to surrender my life and prayers to His will, and that's when I began to really experience joy in prayer.

There is an incredible promise in the book of Isaiah regarding enjoyable prayer.

> "These I will bring to my holy mountain, and make them joyful in my house of prayer..." Isaiah 56:7

This promise is amazing because God promises you joy as you pray. I would suspect that you are like me and struggle at times (or all the time) to enjoy prayer. Most Christians believe prayer is important. Some have faith that it is powerful and effective. But is it enjoyable? That is an entirely different question. Yet this is what God has promised to His people. And I believe His Word provides keys on how to experience that joy.

There are significant practical ways I have experienced greater joy in prayer that we discuss throughout this book — things like combining prayer with musical worship, praying from Scripture and praying in community. But without a doubt, the primary key to enjoyable prayer is intimacy with God. Jesus' first commandment is loving God, and the priority of prayer is intimacy with God.

Intimacy with God through Prayer

The word "intimacy" can be challenging for some people, and I want to address that concern. It may be more comfortable to think of God as your Creator, your Lord and your Savior. These are proper ways to view God, but they do not require that you know Him intimately or even love Him personally. These understandings of God only require that you respect Him, obey Him and believe in Him. But it can be more uncomfortable for some people when you start to speak about love and especially intimacy. Yet the Bible also describes God in intimate, relational terms such as Father, Bridegroom and Friend[10].

When I speak of intimacy with God, I want to be clear that I am not talking about anything sensual. This is about love in your heart. Intimacy emphasizes the personal, emotional and relational connection that God desires to have with you in the deepest place of your being. To be intimate with God is to be fully known by God and to fully know Him. This requires a mutual disclosure of your hearts to one another.

I speak of intimacy with God because it is even more specific than the idea of love. The truth is, you can love someone who doesn't love you in return. God loves many people who do not love Him back. However, experiencing intimacy requires mutual love. Intimacy is voluntarily opening our hearts fully, honestly and vulnerably to God. God will not force this upon you. He gives you a choice. His heart is open to you, but you choose if you will open yourself to Him.

---

10 John 15:15

Intimate prayer is raw prayer. God is not interested in your platitudes and surface-level rhetoric. The truth is, he knows if you are being honest. He knows if you are hiding or holding back your heart to Him. He's patiently waiting for you to come to Him as you are. Prayer filled with religious phrases that are detached from a heart of love are "empty" or "vain" to God[11]. God can handle your sloppy, profanity-laced, confusing, and angry prayers if they are authentic. Your weak and messy prayers do not bother God.

The book of Psalms is full of beautiful examples of God's people coming to Him vulnerably. In fact, learning to pray and sing through the Psalms may be a doorway into greater intimacy with God for you. Many of the Psalms read like journal entries where the writer's hearts bleed onto the pages. King David, the author of most of the Psalms, was imperfect and broken like all of us, but he learned the art of bringing his pain, frustrations, and troubles to God in prayer to cultivate intimacy with God through his struggles. You may be tempted to try to deal with your own problems before you come to God, rather than bringing them to Him. In doing so, you hold back some of who you are from Him and hinder the intimate connection He wants with you. If you are going to pray, be real with God.

The Oil of Intimacy

As a bridegroom pursues His bride, so Jesus is pursuing us. He beckons us to draw near to Him in love. As the lover of Song of Solomon spoke to his beloved, Jesus speaks to us:

"Arise, my love, my beautiful one, and come away."[12]

Will you respond to this call? Will you open your heart to Him? Are you content with lifeless religiosity or do you want

---

11 See Matthew 6:7
12 Song of Solomon 2:13

the joy of true intimacy? Your response to God's invitation to a loving relationship with Him is the most important decision you will ever make.

Jesus gave a parable to illustrate the gravity of our response. In Matthew 25, He describes ten virgins who are awaiting the return of a bridegroom. This symbolizes the return of Jesus, the bridegroom King who is coming again. The virgins fell asleep, and when the alarm sounded that the bridegroom had returned at midnight, only five of the virgins had oil in their lamps. Those who did not were trying to borrow oil from those whose lamps were full, but it was too late. Those with oil in their lamps were invited into the wedding feast, which represented the kingdom of God. To those without oil, the bridegroom said soberly:

> 'Truly, I say to you, I do not know you.'[13]

Jesus made it clear that the oil represents an intimate, prayerful relationship with Him. It is those who *know* Jesus the bridegroom who are invited into the kingdom of God when He returns to the earth. Those who do not know Him are the ones who do not have oil in their lamps. God is now graciously inviting you and me to fill our lamps with the oil of intimacy. This cultivation of intimacy only happens through prayer! Those who pray — truly, intimately, lovingly pray — are those with oil. And you cannot borrow oil from others. Sermons, church attendance, podcasts, books, small groups — none of these can replace a personal relationship with God. One can learn truth from others and even receive an impartation of spiritual gifts. But you cannot impart oil. Oil is only received through intimacy with God. To emphasize his point, Jesus concludes the parable with this final admonition:

> *Watch therefore, for you know neither the day nor the hour.*[14]

---

13   Matthew 25:12
14   Matthew 25:13

Watching is a term used throughout Scripture for prayer. To "watch" is to attentively and earnestly pray. The bridegroom is coming again, and when He returns, His Bride will be faithfully praying. "Oily" prayer is not the religious prayer of duty, but the relational prayer of delight. Those with oil are those who love Jesus. Those who long for His kingdom. Those who want to be closer to Him. Those who need His love. So draw near Him. Watch. Pray. Like a bride anticipating her wedding day, position yourself in prayerful anticipation for Jesus to come again.

This is exactly what you find in the final scenes of the biblical narrative — a wedding day.[15] Every "happily ever after" story points to this ultimate ending. That is why, despite being cliche, the message of eternal bliss resonates so universally. Deep down we all know that the whole point of life is to experience true love. Every wedding on earth foreshadows that ultimate day when the two will become one at the "marriage of the Lamb."[16] It's all about love.

---

15 Revelation 19-22
16 Revelation 19:7

OUR FATHER: THE OBJECT OF PRAYER

A.W. Tozer said that what comes to our minds when we think about God is the most important thing about us[1]. Knowing *who* we are praying to is more important than knowing *how* to pray. If prayer is communication with God, then our view of God profoundly affects our ability to communicate well with him. Perhaps that is why Jesus began his most famous prayer, often called the Lord's Prayer, in Matthew 6:9 with "Our Father." He wanted us to know the One to whom we are praying, not just the correct language to use. He wanted to introduce us to His Father.

In Luke 11, Jesus's disciples had the unique experience of witnessing the incarnate Son of God praying to the Father[2]. It would have been incredible to be present at that moment. We get small glimpses of Jesus's earthly prayer life in the Gospels, but being there in person would have been life-changing. When Jesus was done praying, the only thing the disciples knew to say was "Lord, teach us to pray."[3] When they encountered God talking to God, they realized they did not truly know how to pray. Without hesitation, Jesus said:

---

[1] *The Knowledge of the Holy*, AW Tozer, pg 1
[2] Luke 11:1
[3] Luke 11:2

TWO

When you pray, say: "Father" [4]

I believe this one word is the most important word in the Lord's prayer. Father. Jesus did not encourage His disciples to address God as their "King" or "Lord" or "Creator." These are all aspects of how God relates to us. But Jesus surprisingly encouraged them to approach prayer the way a child talks to a parent. What is it about the nature of a Father that is important to how we pray and relate to God?

Challenges to Seeing God as a Father

For many of us, speaking to God as a Father will bring up mixed emotions. The idea of a "father" may evoke a variety of good and bad memories, depending on your upbringing and experience with your earthly father. To some, the idea of viewing God as our dad is actually painful. That is because we are all wounded by our earthly fathers who are imperfect and prone to human weakness. Even the best human dad will make many mistakes that hurt his children along the way. And the worst fathers can leave deep physical, mental, and emotional wounds from trauma that take years to heal.

To see God as our Father, you must go on a journey of dealing with your own childhood experiences. You need to sort through painful memories and learn to recognize any lies you have believed arising from the inadequacies of your earthly father (or father figures in your life). You will need to forgive. You will need the Holy Spirit to help you know and see what's really going on in your soul. And ultimately, you must renounce the lies you have believed and accept the truth of God's Word about who He really is and who you really are in Him.

This process can be complex and may require assistance from a pastor or trained counselor. Some churches offer "inner healing"

---

[4] Luke 11:2

ministry from individuals trained in helping people work through these kinds of things in a Spirit-led and biblical way. You may want to get additional resources that will guide you through the needed process with more depth and clarity.[5]

But I urge you to take the time to deal with anything in your heart, mind and soul that may be a hindrance to understanding God as a good and loving Father. Your view of God will be distorted by unbiblical lies you have accepted, even subconsciously. They will negatively impact your prayer life, your intimacy with God, and your personal relationships.

As you continue to study the nature of God as our Father, certain lies may be exposed. When that happens, simply renounce them (I suggest doing so out loud) and speak the truth of God's word. I believe God's fierce love has the power to cut through any wounds, pain, trauma, and lies in your life. He can heal you, set you free, and make you new again. This will be a process. I don't expect any of you to have renounced every lie and fully embraced the Fathers' love by the end of this chapter. But you can begin a lifelong journey of freedom. Don't be frustrated if it feels slow. And again, please consider reaching out for help from pastors, a trusted inner healing ministry, and/or professional counseling, as needed.

Confronting Lies About the Father

I was raised by two Christian parents who were married until the death of my father. I was not abused or neglected. We had a great middle-class upbringing in North Carolina with friends, education, sports, music, and all the things you would expect for a healthy childhood. Yet even a fantastic childhood leaves wounds. Parents make mistakes. And while I do not have a lot of traumatic

---

[5] Two books that have helped me are *Receiving Love* by Biuso & Newman, *Experiencing Father's Embrace* by Jack Frost.

childhood memories, I do have painful ones. There are moments where, even if my parents did something right, I perceived their actions in a way that wounded my heart. In those situations, I made a vow or believed a lie that began to shape my worldview even into adulthood. I'll share some examples from my journey to give you context.[6]

Growing up, my brother and I were occasionally spanked for our bad behavior. My dad would often use a wooden ruler. There was one ruler in our home that had a metal edge to it. It was a more expensive ruler, and the metal edge made it easier to draw a good straight line. If Dad spanked one of us with this ruler and it caught our "bottom" the wrong way, it would inflict extra pain and sometimes even break the skin. After pleading with my dad not to use that particular ruler anymore, he promised my brother and me that he would avoid it.

Shortly after this time, my friend Adam had come over to the house to play. We wanted to play outside, but my mom said to stay inside the house. We had the bright idea to disobey my mother and go outside through the window. We were about as sneaky as most elementary aged boys are, and we ended up breaking a window in our attempt to get out of the house.

As expected, my dad was furious and proceeded to grab the nearest ruler (which happened to be the one with the metal edge) to dispense some much-needed discipline for my foolishness. While the spanking hurt, what hurt even more was the fact that he had broken his promise. In retrospect, I can understand my dad's perspective. I had broken the window, which would cost him hundreds of dollars and cause him lots of trouble. He wasn't thinking about which specific ruler he was grabbing. He just

---

[6] I am not a counselor or therapist, so I share my stories only as an example of how God can heal wounds from our pasts. My story is meant to be descriptive, not prescriptive.

wanted to deal with the situation. But as a young boy, this instance wounded me in a particular way.

You don't always know why a certain moment becomes a marking moment in your life. You can't predict why something a person says or does becomes lodged in your soul. But you have certain memories that never leave you. They shape your approach to life, consciously and unconsciously. And maturity requires that you take the time to explore these memories and the beliefs you developed because of them.

My dad had broken his promise. I had gone too far, and so he hurt me. Honestly, this probably wasn't the only time my dad inadvertently broke a promise or went back on his word. But it is the one I remember. It was a key moment that caused me to question things:

Can anyone be trusted? Will anyone keep their promises? Will God keep His promises? Maybe He will as long as I'm good. I need to be perfect so I don't get hurt. If I sin too much, God will lose his temper, get mad and hurt me. I need to put my guard up and be suspicious. I don't want to ever trust anyone too deeply, because it might bite me in the back. Etc.

I was obviously not self-aware enough as a child to understand that I was building an entire belief system off this experience. At the moment, I was simply hurt and trying to cope. Yet as I went through life, the lie (that I can't trust people) continued to come along with me, impacting my relationship with God and others.

The truth that I had to learn to accept is that God can be trusted. The Father does keep His promises. He is slow to anger and rich in love.

Over the years, as the Holy Spirit has brought multiple painful memories to my mind, I have been able to identify the lies that accompanied them and receive the biblical truths about my heavenly Father.

What comes to mind when we think about God as Father? Most of us have filters from our past that taint our understanding of who He really is and how we should relate to Him. We must allow the truth of God as Father to set us free and draw us into joyful prayer. Let's dive into some of the truths about our Father in heaven.

The Father Pursues Us In Love

Perhaps the most illuminating revelation that Jesus gives about God as our Father is nestled in the parable commonly known as the Prodigal Son[7]. The story begins with a father and two sons. One of the sons decided that he wanted to get his inheritance early in order to leave home and be on his own.

After squandering his money on lavish (i.e. "prodigal") living, he found himself feeding pigs, which were unclean animals for the Jewish people. He was so hungry that he ate out of the pig trough, which would have been not only humiliating and gross but also utterly sinful. Finally, the son came to the end of himself and decided it would be better to return home as a slave to his father than to continue in his current situation.

The son expected condemnation and rejection. He anticipated the need to beg for an opportunity to even be a servant in the household. He was stinky, dirty, broke, embarrassed, and exhausted. Jesus described what happened next:

> "But while he was still a long way off, his father saw him and was filled with compassion for him; he ran to his son, threw his arms around him and kissed him." Luke 15:20

Rather than condemnation, the son received love. Rather than begging for acceptance, the father ran to the son and embraced him. The son tried to start his rehearsed apology, but the father

---

[7] Luke 15:11-32

totally ignored him and started throwing a party to celebrate the child's return.

The older brother, who had stayed at home the entire time, became jealous of the way the younger brother was being treated. He became resentful about the grace being shown by his father, and he refused to come into the home during the celebration. Again, we see the father moving in love towards one of his sons. He went outside the house, pleaded for reconciliation with his older son, and reaffirmed his love and acceptance.

This beautiful story captures the heart of the Father who we come to in prayer. He is a Father who pursues us in love. He is a Father who is patient with us. He is gracious. He does not condemn us when we come to Him after a mistake. We do not have to earn our way back into His presence. Jesus has earned our way into the Father's house for us. All we have to do is keep returning to Him.

God Rejoices Over Us

We are all tempted to be like both of these brothers. We are all tempted by either rebellion or religion.[8] The younger brother was rebellious. He abandoned his father's house and embraced licentious living. The older brother was religious. He seemed to be faithful to the father, but the end of the story reveals the truth of his heart. He thought he was earning his place at the father's house by his good works. Neither son understood the heart of their father.

Don't forget the truth of the gospel. It is the blood of Jesus that cleanses your sin and makes a way for you to enter the kingdom of God. Your good works don't save you and your sins do not condemn you. Trust in the work of Christ on the cross

---

[8] I borrowed this terminology from Mark Driscoll. See https://realfaith.com/sermons/the-parable-of-the-prodigal-son/

as your salvation. It is the death and resurrection of Jesus that reveals to you the heart of the Father. In sending His Son to die, the Father ran after you, even while you were "a long way off" in your sins.

> But God shows his love for us in that while we were still sinners, Christ died for us. Romans 5:8

When you pray "our Father," you are praying to the kind of father who pursues you while you're still in your sin. You are praying to a Father who embraces you while you still stink. You are praying to a Father who celebrates and rejoices every time you turn our heart to Him. You are praying to a Father who does not demand that you earn your way into His house. When you put your faith in Christ, He welcomes you, just as you are, to become a child of God. And for those who are in Christ, there is now no condemnation.[9]

Even when you continue to make mistakes, you can "come home" to the Father, confess your sins, and know that He is always waiting with open arms. This does not mean that you can be flippant about sin, but it gives you assurance that, regardless of your sin, you are His son or daughter. He always loves you, and His kindness will lead you to repentance. You don't need to try to self-righteously "fix" yourself before going to Him. You can go to Him as you are, and He receives you, loves you, and helps you grow in maturity.

I encourage you to use a sanctified imagination in prayer. Close your eyes and imagine the Father. When you speak to Him, what's happening? What is the look on His face? What is His body language communicating to you about His heart? This parable Jesus told shows you just what you need to imagine. The Father

---

9   Romans 8:1

is smiling. He is running to you with His arms open wide. He is happy to see you when you come to Him. He rejoices over you.

If you have any contradictory ideas about God as you imagine coming into His presence, they are not based on truth. God is not grumpy. He is not angry with you. He is not frustrated or exasperated. He is not resentful or bitter. His arms are not crossed. His finger is not wagging. His eyes are not rolling. He is tender and kind. He is patient and compassionate. He is full of joy and life and energy and peace. The Bible describes God as literally dancing and singing over His people.

> *The Lord your God is in your midst, a mighty one who will save; he will rejoice [ie dance] over you with gladness; he will quiet you by his love; he will exult over you with loud singing. Zephaniah 3:17*

Can you imagine a God who starts dancing and singing when you approach Him? Is this your typical mindset when you pray? When you say, "Our Father," do you smell the fatted calf on the fire? Do you hear the song of the joyful Father? Do you sense His delight for you? Do you know that you're coming into His presence as a rightful heir and child? Do you come boldly as a son or daughter?

The Fellowship of the Trinity

The Bible teaches us that we worship a God who is three persons in One. The Father, the Son and the Holy Spirit are "one in essence." It is important to understand the Father in this context. The complexity of the doctrine known as the "Trinity" is a mystery to our finite minds. However, what God has shown to us about His Trinitarian nature reveals that He is relational and familial to His very core. The Father, Son, and Holy Spirit eternally relate to one another in pure and holy love within the person of God. The Father loves the Son and Spirit. The Son loves the Father and the Spirit. The Spirit loves the Father and the Son. This explains how God *is* love in Himself.[10]

When Jesus encourages you to pray to God as a Father, He is actually inviting you to relate to God the Father as He relates to the Father. This is profound! You are invited into the eternal love relationship that flows within the Godhead. The same passion, joy, pleasure, and delight that is in God's self-sustaining heart can be experienced by weak people like you and me. This is the opportunity you have in prayer.

In this light, prayer becomes far more than getting your needs met or fulfilling a religious obligation. You were made to pray because you were made to know God. God is relational, and you are made in His image. Jesus' burning desire is for you to come into His presence, behold His glory and experience the ecstasy of Trinitarian love. One of the few times you do get to see what Jesus is praying to the Father, you see him pleading for this very thing.

> *Father, I desire that they also, whom you have given me, may be with me where I am, to see my glory that you have given me because you loved me before the foundation of the world. John 17:24*

Jesus is praying this for us.[11] He is asking the Father for us to be with Him and to experience the love of the Father that He experiences as the Son. And I assure you — Jesus's prayer will be answered. We the Church will come to know God as our Father. All the lies will be obliterated with the truth. All the wounds will be healed. All the barriers to knowing God's heart, seeing Him

---

10   I John 4:8
11   "I do not ask for these only, but also for those who will believe in me through their word" John 17:20

rightly, and experiencing His love will be removed as the Holy Spirit pours His love into our hearts.[12]

This is the desire of Jesus for you. This is how He teaches you to pray. Pray to a Father who loves you and wants you to be close to Him. Pray to a God who is inviting you as close as possible. This Father desires your intimacy so much that He sent His only begotten Son to the earth to die on a cross to also have you as his son or daughter. What a love! What a Father!

A Special Note About This Chapter

The information in this chapter and the next were originally going to be one section of a chapter about the Lord's Prayer. Yet as I wrote, the words kept coming. I realized God was speaking in an unexpected way about His desire for us to approach Him the way a child comes to a loving Father.

Not only did I sense the Holy Spirit flowing through me in an unexpected way as I wrote, but the circumstances of my life added to the gravity of what God was speaking. About two-thirds of the way through writing this manuscript, my dad was admitted to the hospital after falling a few times at home. He had unknowingly suffered a few small strokes. His health crisis threw a wrench into my writing timeline.

A few months later, towards the end of April, I was finally able to muster up the energy to write again. However, about a week later, my dad went back into the hospital. This time it was cancer, and he passed away in less than a month.

I have had to embrace God as my Father in a new way during this season of my life, now that I no longer have an earthly father. Despite the grief and setbacks of this season, I can't help but see the timing of it all as providential. As the Holy Spirit was leading me to write extensively about the importance of coming to God

---
[12] Romans 5:5

as our Father and knowing our identity as His children, my earthly dad was passing away. God is quite an author Himself, and I was keenly aware of Him authoring the story of my life as I wrote this book — especially these chapters.

When God goes out of His way to get your attention, it is because He wants to speak clearly to you. Just as God is crafting a poetic storyline surrounding the production of this book, He is also writing your story. He wants to speak to you. And it seems He really wants you to know Him as a Father and understand your identity as His son or daughter.

SONSHIP: OUR IDENTITY IN PRAYER

My wife Shepard woke me up around three a.m. Her water broke. Our first child would soon be born. Adrenaline kicked in as I threw on my clothes, helped Shepard to the car, and rushed her to the hospital. Our first-born daughter Shiloh arrived just before the sun was up. Her birthday was on Sunday the thirteenth, just like mine. She came quickly in the early morning hours, and she has continued to do everything early and quickly her entire life. She's an early riser, fast talker, and quick learner.

It is hard to describe the feeling of becoming a new parent. I felt proud, confused, overwhelmed, exhausted, protective, and delighted all at once. Actually, Shiloh later created the word "nervited" to describe when she feels both nervous and happily excited, and I think that's the perfect way to describe it. I felt extremely nervited when she was born.

I clearly recall one distinct impulse that rose in my heart shortly after her birth. I wanted to get everyone's attention, raise my voice, and proudly display my new daughter for everyone to see — like Mufasa holding up baby Simba in *The Lion King*. She was my kid, and I wanted everyone to know it! She hadn't done a thing for me, but she had my whole heart. In fact, she had already cost us time, energy, and money. But she could not have earned our love anyway. We love her because she is ours, not because of something she does (or does not do) for us. No three a.m. wake up call, dirty diaper, toddler tantrum, or sassy attitude has deterred us from loving her unconditionally.

After Shiloh we had three more beautiful children, and I can confirm that the impulses to wildly love and celebrate our children arose every time a new one entered our world. God has used the process of having children to show me His Father's heart in many ways. I have such a deep love for my own kids that it is hard to believe that God loves me (and everyone) infinitely more than that. In becoming a father, I've learned over and over again how to be God's son. He is proud of me. He loves me unconditionally. I belong to Him. And He loves me just because I'm His son. Like a newborn baby who has yet to do anything for their parents, I come to God in my emptiness and still receive extravagant acceptance and affection from the Father.

> See what kind of love the Father has given to us, that we should be called children of God; and so we are. I John 3:1

Our Identity as Sons and Daughters

When Jesus taught his disciples to pray to God as Father, he brought revelation regarding the nature of God, but He also brought revelation about their identity in Him. If God was their Father, that meant that they were sons of God. If God is Father, then you are a son or daughter. If you are not willing to accept this truth, you will find yourself falling back into bad habits again and again. You will start believing lies that will hijack your good intentions. You will start praying as if you are a slave or orphan, instead of talking to the Lord as His child.

In Jesus's parable[1] we discussed last chapter, the younger brother had lost his identity as a son. He had mistakenly begun

---
[1] See the discussion of the Prodigal Son parable of Luke 15 in the previous chapter.

to believe that his identity was based on his performance. He even proposed becoming a slave of his father when he returned home. The Father's gracious response to him reminded him that he was a son because of his identity, not because of what he did or didn't do.

The older son was just as confused. His identity was not rooted in his mistakes but rooted in his (apparent) goodness. However, the underlying issue was still there. His identity was based on his performance. He thought he deserved to be a son because he had been faithful to his father and worked hard for years. He forgot that his sonship was based on his father's love, not his own good deeds.

If your identity is based on your performance, then your sense of worth will rise and fall with your sense of good and bad behavior. On seemingly "good" days, you will be arrogant and on your seemingly "bad" days, you will feel condemned. But a son or daughter whose identity is rooted in the Father's love is free from the roller coaster of performance-based-identity. There is a stability that comes because you know that your sonship is based on the work of Jesus and not your own works, good or bad.

Clarity regarding your identity requires revelation by the Spirit of God from the truth of Scripture and experiential encounter with the heart of the Father. It takes the Holy Spirit to reveal these things to your heart. I encourage you to take time today to ask the Holy Spirit to reveal the heart of the Father to you. Invite Him to baptize you in His love and power. Pray Ephesians 3:16-19 over your own heart:

> *"...through his Spirit in your inner being... you, being rooted and grounded in love, may have strength to comprehend with all the saints what is the breadth and length and height and depth, and to know the love of Christ that*

> *surpasses knowledge, that you may be filled with all the fullness of God."*

The prayer to be "rooted and grounded" in love is a prayer for certainty and confidence in God's love for you. God wants to reveal His love as a Father so profoundly that "you know that you know" that you are His child and that He is a good Father who loves you. Being rooted in this love keeps you steady on good days and bad days. Criticism doesn't derail you. Your own mistakes don't derail you. Your own successes don't puff you up with pride. Relational challenges don't send you into a tailspin. Because when everything around you is swirling with inconsistency, you have a constant anchor for your soul: the Father loves you. You are his child. And nothing can change that.

These truths are true whether you believe them or not. His love is a reality whether you accept it or not. But I believe God wants you to experience it. When the apostle Paul prays that the church would "comprehend" God's love[2], that word means to "catch or lay hold of" something. There is something tangible about this understanding. Can you really know love without experiencing it? Can you explain love to someone who has never tasted it? How do you comprehend God's love except that you feel it? I believe God wants you to know the truth of His love in your mind and to feel His love in your soul.

Yet you must be honest that there are days you don't feel it. There are days you feel far from God, don't feel His presence, don't hear His voice, and don't recognize His touch. In moments where you are struggling, how do you stay rooted and grounded in His love? In seasons where you don't feel His love experientially, how can you stay confident in your identity as His child? In the age to come, you will experience unhindered access to the unfiltered love

---

2 Ephesians 3:18

and glory of God. But in this age, you only experience a measure of His presence. You see in a mirror dimly.[3] The kingdom is now but not yet.[4] So how do you walk in your identity during the "not yet" seasons?

This is when you remember the gospel. The greatest expression of the Father's love for you is that He sent His son to die on the cross. This is the ultimate revelation of the heart of our Father. Jesus came over 2,000 years ago. What He has already done for you is proof of the love of God. God does not need to do anything else. You can know He loves you because Jesus came. Jesus died. And Jesus rose again.

> *For God so loved the world, that he gave his only Son, that whoever believes in him should not perish but have eternal life. John 3:16*

The gospel is your anchor. God so loved the world that He gave Jesus. Even when you don't feel it, you can know it is the truth. On good days and bad days, it remains the same. God loves you. He is your Father, and you are His child. As a son or daughter, you are a rightful heir of the kingdom of God in Christ.[5] This is your portion. This is your inheritance. This is who you are.

Born Again and Adopted

When the Bible describes you as a child of God, it uses two different metaphors to explain that relationship. You are both born of God and adopted by God. Unlike earthly children who are either adopted by their parents or born of their parents, God's heavenly children are both at the same time. You are a rightful

---

3   I Corinthians 13:12
4   I discuss this concept more in chapter 12 of my book *David's Tabernacle: How God's Presence Changes Everything*
5   Romans 8:17

heir in the family of God who has been born again by the Spirit of God. At the same time, you are chosen and adopted by God.

When the Pharisee Nicodemus approached Jesus in the night, Jesus described the conditions required to enter the kingdom of God. He declared that anyone who wants to enter must be "born again"[6] and unless one is "born of water and the Spirit"[7] they will never gain entrance into God's kingdom. This foreshadowed Jesus's death and resurrection. Just as Christ died and came back to life, so those who follow Him must die to their sins and be resurrected in new life. This is what baptism represents[8]. The apostle Peter used the same terminology of being "born again" in his first letter[9].

A Christian is born again spiritually as a "new creation"[10] in Christ Jesus. You receive a "new heart and a new spirit"[11] inside your being. You are ultimately and foundationally transformed from the inside out. It's not just that God the Father becomes your legal guardian when you are saved. Christians are "partakers of the divine nature"[12]. Adopted children do not carry their parents' DNA and will therefore not have the same innate tendency to be like their parents to the degree that a naturally born child will. But as a child born of God, you will inevitably reflect the nature of your Father as you grow and mature. When you put your faith in Christ, you were born of God's Spirit and received new spiritual DNA. From the core of your being, you are truly His son or daughter.

6	John 3:3, 7
7	John 3:5-6
8	Romans 6:4
9	I Peter 1:3, 23
10	2 Corinthians 5:17
11	Ezekiel 36:26
12	2 Peter 1:4

Not only are you born again into the family of God, but you have been adopted into the family of God. This reveals another facet of what it means to be God's child. A mother and father do not choose their natural-born children. They simply receive the child that comes from the womb as a gift from God, with its unique gifts, beauty, flaws, personality, and quirks. It is true that modern science is trying to play God and allow parents to tweak the genes of their children, but parents who simply allow God to be God will be blessed with whatever kind of child that arrives on the day it is born.

To say it crudely, parents are stuck with their children. Regardless of the quality of the relationship, there is still an inescapable biological connection between a parent and a child. A simple DNA test can prove it. Yet a biological connection does not indicate a loving relationship. Anyone with an estranged relationship with a parent or child is aware of this reality. But is this the nature of our relationship to God? Do we simply "carry his DNA"? Is the Father "stuck" with us? Of course not.

There is another dimension to God's love and fathering that is completely unique. You are not only born of God but you are also adopted by God. God chooses you. He wants you to be His kid. He sees you, knows you, and still decides to draw closer. He knows what He is getting into, but He is not deterred. He knows your thoughts, your decisions, your personality, your weaknesses, your failures,[13] and despite it all… He has chosen you to be His child and carry His name.

The Spirit of Adoption

In the same passage where the apostle Paul describes us as "heirs" of God's promises, He also describes the Holy Spirit as

---

13 See Psalm 139:2-4

the Spirit of adoption[14] who confirms our identity as children of God. The Holy Spirit dwells in your heart when you first accept Christ,[15] and He continues to fill you more and more.[16] And part of the work of the Holy Spirit inside you is to confirm and clarify your identity as an adopted child in God's family. This passage says that the Spirit inside you is who causes you to cry out to God as a Father.

> *For you did not receive the spirit of slavery to fall back into fear, but you have received the Spirit of adoption as sons, by whom we cry, "Abba! Father!" The Spirit himself bears witness with our spirit that we are children of God, and if children, then heirs—heirs of God and fellow heirs with Christ, provided we suffer with him in order that we may also be glorified with him. Romans 8:15-17*

If you are to pray to God as your Father, like Jesus instructed, then you must be filled with the Holy Spirit of adoption. You must invite and welcome the Spirit of God to baptize you, fill you, and consume you with His presence and power. You must welcome His voice to affirm your identity in Him and to reveal more of God's love to your heart.[17] You were born again of the Holy Spirit, and your adoption is sealed by the Holy Spirit.

God has chosen you. While God does not "decide" to do anything in the same way we decide, you can rest assured that He is not adopting you begrudgingly. His heart's desire is to know you, love you, and be your Father. You are His delight and desire. The greatest love of any parent on earth is a small reflection of the perfect love of our heavenly Father.

---

14 Romans 8:15
15 Ephesians 1:13
16 Ephesians 5:18
17 Romans 5:5

> *If you then, who are evil, know how to give good gifts to your children, how much more will the heavenly Father give the Holy Spirit to those who ask him!" Luke 11:13*

The apostle Paul describes the church in Colossae as "God's chosen ones"[18] and Peter calls the church a "chosen generation"[19]. A common New Testament term for God's people is "the elect"[20], which literally means the chosen ones. This is who you are. You are chosen and adopted by God. The fact that you are chosen also speaks to your identity as part of the bride of Christ — a people chosen by Jesus as His eternal partner.

Avoiding An Orphan or Slave Mentality

If you are adopted by God, then before you decided to follow Jesus you were an orphan. Before putting your faith in Christ you were alone, without a spiritual family. If the "Spirit of adoption" provides identity, freedom, love, a home, and acceptance, then your pre-Christian "orphan spirit" filled you with confusion, bondage, fear, loneliness, and rejection. Jesus understood our condition and promised to give you the Holy Spirit to set you free from this orphan mentality that tormented you because of sin.

> *"I will not leave you as orphans; I will come to you." John 14:18*

When we come to God in prayer, we must know who we are. When we go forward into the world to fulfill God's purposes for our lives, we must know who we are. We are no longer orphans. We are no longer slaves. The body of Christ must rise in confidence as the Father's beloved children. Could it be that this is what an enslaved, orphaned world is longing to see?[21]

18	Colossians 3:12
19	I Peter 2:9
20	Including in one of Jesus' key teachings on prayer in Luke 18:7
21	Romans 8:19

As long as you are deceived by the mindset of a slave or orphan, you will never learn to enjoy prayer as God designed it. Even though you are truly a child of God, the enemy will still try to lie to you concerning who God is and who you really are in Him. The enemy comes with lies to deceive you, and you must be ready to take every thought captive[22]. Below are some common signs of having either an orphan or slave mentality. Understanding these signs can help you expose the work of the enemy in your heart and mind.

Some signs that you may struggle with an orphan mindset are:
- You are independent and self-reliant
- You carry a fear of abandonment
- You feel lonely
- You have trouble trusting and committing

Some signs that you may struggle with a slave mindset are:
- You can't easily celebrate other people's victories
- You are easily jealous
- You may be committed to church & ministry, but are religious, proud, and self-righteous
- You suffer from condemnation and shame
- You can't ever rest, receive, and relax

Many of these tendencies overlap, and everybody will struggle with some of them occasionally. When you look back at the Prodigal Son story, you probably see glimpses of yourself in both the older and younger brother. The point is not to label yourself or create needless categories. The goal is to expose the enemy's lies so that you can receive the truth of God's Word regarding His love for you as a Father and your identity in Christ as His child. Don't worry as much if you tend to act like an "older brother,"

---

[22] 2 Corinthians 10:4-6

"younger brother," "orphan," or "slave." The truth will set you free.[23] God is your Father, you are His child, and He loves you. Receive it!

---

[23] John 8:32

FIRST: THE PRIORITY OF PRAYER

When one of our daughters was young, she wanted to help us water plants in our yard. The large bushes had leaves growing nearly as tall as her. It seemed most natural to her to water the big foliage right in front of her face. She picked up the watering can and began dumping water over the top of the plants, spilling much of it on the ground, the sidewalk, and her own clothes. She didn't understand that the roots needed water, not the fruit.

The visible part of the bush was only a fraction of the entire plant. Underneath the surface of the earth, an intricate, hidden root system pulled in water and nutrients that nourished the parts of the plant we could see. We had to teach her to soak the base of the plant, so water would reach the roots. If the roots were watered, then the plant would be healthy and grow.

Many of us approach our spiritual lives the same way my daughter approached our bushes. We get focused on what is outward and visible, while ignoring what is under the surface.

Jesus taught about prayer and intimacy using the analogy of a plant bearing fruit. Just like a plant, our spiritual roots must be connected to the nourishment of His love and word in order to help us be healthy and grow. Christians who are wise learn from

Jesus, prioritize intimacy with Him and bear long-term fruit in their lives.

> *I am the vine; you are the branches. Whoever abides in me and I in him, he it is that bears much fruit, for apart from me you can do nothing. John 15:5*

Jesus said He was the vine and the disciples were the branches. Unless the disciples stayed connected to Jesus in intimacy, through prayer and His word, then they would not bear fruit in their lives. Their capacity to be used by God to impact the world for the sake of God's kingdom was based on their willingness to stay rooted to God in intimacy. Jesus then made one of the most stunning statements in the Bible: "Apart from me you can do nothing."

Jesus clearly emphasized the priority of having a relationship with Him. Putting anything before Jesus results in "nothing." Nothing that lasts. Nothing that has any eternal impact. Nothing that really means anything. Only things that result from the overflow of first knowing God are what matter. The fruit of a meaningful life grows from the root of intimacy with the Lord. Jesus describes this fruit as that which "remains" or "abides."[1]

Don't you want to live a life that leaves a legacy? Don't you want to positively impact future generations? Don't you want your efforts, energy, and time to go towards something that really matters? Don't you want a fruitful life? There is only one way. Abide in Christ. Abide in His presence. Abide in His word. Abide in prayer.

It is important to look at the place of prayer in the priorities of your life. We are all balancing the busyness of jobs, school, families, friends, and hobbies. Where does prayer fit into the calendars? If there is a conflict, what takes top priority? We know

---

[1] See John 15:16

we should abide in God through prayer, but it is easy to let it fall to the wayside as you get caught up in the activity of your days.

> *"I have so much to do that I shall spend the first three hours in prayer"* - Martin Luther[2]

My encouragement to prioritize prayer in this chapter is not a discouragement against any other Christian ministry work or healthy activity in life. Some people promote a particular ministry activity by downplaying the importance of another activity. That is not my goal here. The Bible highlights many important things for the Lord's people. Our spouses and children are important. Our involvement in church life is important. Our integrity and hard work at a vocation is important. Our friendships and fellowship with other believers are important. Using our spiritual gifts is important. Evangelism is important. Caring for the poor is important. Global missions is important. Being involved in the government is important. Rest and recreation are important. I could go on and on.

My emphasis on prayer is not to disregard any of the many things that the Scriptures describe as important to God. My claim in this chapter is simply this: *Your relationship with God is the most important thing in your life, and therefore — prayer being one of the primary ways you relate to God — prayer should be prioritized.*

Your relationship with God is the root that provides your soul nourishment, life, discernment, direction, energy, peace, power and all that you need to do all the many things God has called you to do. It's not that you should pray instead of doing other things. Rather, you need to pray in order to do all the other things well.

---

2 https://books.google.com/books?id=nKRVAAAAYAAJ&dq=%22spend%20the%20first%20three%20hours%20in%20prayer%22&pg=PA221#v=onepage&q&f=false

FOUR

The Priority of Prayer in Jesus's Life

Jesus is our prime example of a lifestyle of prayer and intimacy with the Father. His entire earthly ministry was launched out of a 40-day season of fasting and prayer. He would often withdraw to spend time with the Father. He would stay up late or get up early to spend more time in prayer. And he taught his disciples to do the same.

Because Jesus is God, it is hard to understand why He would need to pray. Yet the Gospels paint a picture of Jesus relating to the Father in prayer consistently. Was this because, in his humanity, Jesus *needed* to pray, just as we do? Was it simply Jesus's desire to get alone with the Father because of His love? Or was Jesus living to be a model for us? The truth is, we can not fully comprehend what was happening when God incarnate was talking to the Father in heaven. We do not know what exactly was going on in Jesus' soul. But I know one thing. If Jesus needed a prayer life, then I do too.

One of the most revealing verses about Jesus' commitment to prayer is in Luke 5:16.

> *So He Himself often withdrew into the wilderness and prayed.*[3]

Jesus made a habit of prayer. He withdrew "often." Despite the demands on His time and the daily challenges of surviving in the first century, Jesus set an example for us as one who withdrew to pray regularly. In fact, the context of this verse indicates that demands on Jesus' time and attention were increasing as his ministry expanded.[4] The preceding verse states "the report went around concerning Him" and "multitudes" were gathering to hear Him preach and receive healing from their infirmities.

---

3   Luke 5:16, NKJV
4   See Luke 5:15

If you applied our modern ministry mindset to Jesus's life, this would be considered an important season of momentum for his ministry efforts. One could assume Jesus would not want to disappear at this key moment of growth and expansion, right? Wouldn't he want to increase his output to meet the growing demands of the people? Shouldn't he strike while the fire is hot? Jesus' ministry was "going viral," yet Luke wants us to know that Jesus continued to prioritize His relationship with His Father through prayer amid the pressure and busyness.

It is almost as if Jesus snuck away to pray specifically *because* there was an increase of demands in his life. Maybe He didn't pray despite the needs but because of them. Perhaps it was his love and compassion for the crowds that provoked His withdrawal. Elsewhere He told his disciples to pray because the harvest was great but the laborers were few[5]. It seems His priority for prayer was not a way to neglect people's needs. Rather, prayer was an important way for Him to minister to others most effectively.

Jesus recognized that the people's needs were so great that his own human soul was going to hit its limits trying to serve everyone. He loved all people, but he knew that, in his humanity, his capacity to meet their needs was limited. Jesus loved the crowds, but He was not led primarily by the needs of those around Him. He was led by the Spirit and the voice of His Father. In John's gospel, He makes a stunning statement about how the Father's voice directed his steps during his life on earth.

> *The Son can do nothing of his own accord, but only what he sees the Father doing. For whatever the Father does, that the Son does likewise. John 5:19*

This verse explains how Jesus could operate with compassion towards people and their needs, without feeling responsible to

---

5   Luke 10:2

meet every need in every moment. The Son looked to the Father for direction and leadership, and He trusted the Father's love for people.

In order to only do "what he sees the Father doing," Jesus had to spend time with His Father — looking and listening through prayer. To do what the Father does, you must first see and know what the Father is doing. Jesus' life of prayer and intimacy allowed Him to walk in perfect lockstep with the heart of the Father. Led by the Spirit, Jesus could discern in each moment what to do and not to do. The very context of this verse gives us an example.

At the beginning of John 5, we see Jesus going to a pool in Bethesda. The passage describes a multitude of people with physical infirmities. Apparently, an angel would come down and the first person to dip in the water would receive healing. Among that large crowd, Jesus focused on one crippled man to talk with. He healed the man, and then, as far as we know, He walked away. He only healed one man in the crowd of sick people. We have no explanation for why He did this, other than the hint that Jesus offered a few verses later: *The Son can do nothing of his own accord, but only what he sees the Father doing.*

With the limitations of His physical human body, Jesus could not do everything Himself (this is why He would later tell His disciples that it was better for Him to go away and send the Holy Spirit to the church[6]). So He had peace about healing only one man in the crowd of infirm people. He loved all people, but crowds did not determine His actions. He was driven primarily by obedience to the Father.

In order to walk in that love and obedience, Jesus had to prioritize time with His Father. He knew that if he abandoned intimacy with the Father, He would no longer have anything to

---

[6] John 14:12,17

offer people. His love relationship with the Father was the oil in the lamp of his ministry that allowed Him to burn bright and hot. There was a direct correlation between staying connected to the Father through prayer and the fruitfulness of his life. So he prayed often.

The Priority of Prayer in the Early Church

The disciples followed Jesus' example. After his death, resurrection, and ascension into heaven, the apostles launched a 10-day prayer meeting in an upper room[7]. Scripture says that they "with one accord were devoting themselves to prayer"[8]. Before departing from the earth, Jesus had urged them to wait for the promise of the Holy Spirit to come upon them[9]. It was the power of the Holy Spirit, received in prayer, that would enable the church to be witnesses of the gospel to the ends of the earth[10].

Jesus also gave the apostles the Great Commission to make disciples throughout the world[11]. He instructed them to *go* to the nations with the good news, but He also told them to *wait* for the promised power. Then Jesus left them. What did they do? Did they *wait* or did they *go*? Did they pray or did they make disciples?

They did both, of course, but they prayed *first*. They gathered in the upper room, devoted themselves to prayer, waited for the outpouring of the Holy Spirit, and then went out to share the gospel with power, signs, and wonders. After ten days of waiting and praying, the Holy Spirit came and filled them. It happened on the day of the Hebrew feast of Pentecost. Peter stood up and preached the gospel and three thousand of those gathered for the feast became Christians. The church was born, and revival began

---

7   Acts 1:12-14
8   Acts 1:14
9   Acts 1:4-8
10   Acts 1:8
11   Matthew 28:19-20

in Jerusalem. I wonder what would have happened if Peter had stood up to preach on the day that Jesus ascended? Certainly not such a great harvest—if any at all. They had to pray first.

Jesus intentionally birthed the church from a prayer meeting. The first occurrence of something in Scripture often sets a pattern for the rest of the Bible. This story of the launch of the early church in Acts 1-2 is no different. God was teaching people His ways, and this same pattern has been repeated throughout two millennia of church history. David Bradshaw says it like this:

> "Over and over, even after this revival on the day of Pentecost, these early believers went to the Temple daily for prayer (Acts 2:46, 3:1). They were locked into a lifestyle of praying together.... I have discovered from the Book of Acts that this pattern is repeated many times, and it only continued."[12]

As if the story of Pentecost was not clear enough, only a few chapters later we find the same believers gathered in prayer again following a time of persecution. It's the Upper Room 2.0. They experienced a great revival, now they experienced great resistance (as expected), and so they followed the pattern. They gathered in united prayer again, God poured out His Spirit again, and they returned to the city boldly proclaiming the word of God again[13].

Ministry to the Lord — through prayer, worship, waiting, and fasting — always leads to ministry to others — discipleship, evangelism, and missions. United, corporate, Spirit-filled prayer was not just the way Christianity began; it is the only way it continues. The church in Jerusalem continued the upper room pattern, and God is calling us to do the same. A praying Church is God's strategy for His kingdom purposes on the earth.

---

12 *Awaken the Dawn*, pg 8-9
13 Acts 4:23-31

To avoid being redundant, I'll avoid working painstakingly through the emphasis on prayer throughout the rest of the book of Acts. Instead, I will offer the highlights below to give you an idea of how important prayer was to the life and mission of the early church.

- As I noted, after Jesus' ascension, the apostles first activity was gathering to pray until Pentecost (Acts 1:14).
- Prayer continued to be one of the primary activities at church gatherings after Pentecost (Acts 2:42).
- The believers in Jerusalem went to the temple to pray together daily at the "hour of prayer" (Acts 3:1, Acts 22:17).
- The church gathered to pray in response to persecution and was baptized in fresh power and boldness to minister to others — Upper Room 2.0 (Acts 4:23-31).
- The apostles found themselves overwhelmed by feeding the poor, so they delegated those responsibilities and returned to prayer and the study of God's word as their primary responsibilities as church leaders (Acts 6:4).
- Christians united in a home to offer "constant prayer" for Peter, even throughout the night (Acts 12:5,12).
- The church gathered to minister to God with worship and prayer in Antioch, the first predominantly Gentile church. The Holy Spirit spoke during the corporate worship, and the first missionaries were sent out to the nations (Acts 13:1-3). The Greek word here for "ministry to the Lord" is *leitourgeō* which is where we get the English word "liturgy" — implying that corporate prayer & worship was an ongoing activity of the church there.
- Leaders in local churches were appointed after a time of prayer and fasting (Acts 14:23).

- At the Jerusalem council, the apostle James spoke to the elders and apostles about the restoration of the tabernacle of David being part of God's strategy for completing the Great Commission in the nations. This includes the restoration of extravagant worship and prayer to the church (Acts 15:16-17).[14]
- The church dedicated certain *times* for prayer (remember the "hour of prayer"), but they also established *places* for prayer. In Philippi a common gathering place for corporate prayer was near the river — an outdoor prayer room! (Acts 16:13,16)
- When Paul and Silas found themselves imprisoned for their faith, they went back to the original pattern. With their backs bloodied and their feet shackled, they begin to sing and pray to the Lord during the night. God released His power, set them free from their chains and allowed them to share the gospel with the jailer and his family (Acts 16:25-34).
- At the furthest extent of his early missionary journey, Paul gathered with the churches at Ephesus and Tyre to pray (Acts 20:36, 21:5). Wherever the gospel spread, praying churches were established.

Many people talk about wanting to get back to the power and fruitfulness of the early church in the book of Acts. I agree that the stories of how the Holy Spirit was moving in the early days of Christianity should convict and inspire us. Yet we may be tempted to pursue God's power before His presence. Remember the story with my daughter watering our plants — we need to focus on the roots if we want to see fruit. We need to pray first, like the early church.

14　See my book *David's Tabernacle: How God's Presence Changes Everything*. I specifically discuss this Acts 15 passage in chapter 13.

I could continue to cite dozens of verses throughout the rest of the New Testament about prayer[15]. Paul exhorted churches to pray in nearly all his letters. John, Peter, Jude, James — each New Testament author speaks about the importance and priority of prayer. Jesus set the example, taught his disciples, and the early church continued to follow in the ways of Christ. Prayer is not the *only* ministry you have as a Christian, but it is your *first* ministry. The biblical pattern is that ministry to the Lord comes before ministry to others. You should prioritize prayer in order to serve and fuel all that God has called you to do. Your relationships, workplace, school, church, city, and nation will all be better if you pray first.

Throughout Christian history, you find that the Christians who impacted the world prioritized prayer. Within a few hundred years after the birth of Christianity, there were communities beginning to take the apostle Paul's exhortation to pray without ceasing[16] literally. The desert fathers and early monks would immerse themselves in lifestyles of contemplative prayer and fasting. Throughout the Middle Ages, monasteries organized 24-hour-a-day prayer watches that lasted for years at a time. All the great reformers, revivalists, and missionaries of the last 500 years were men and women of prayer. Catholic monks and nuns gave themselves to extravagant prayer. Great protestant missions movements were launched and sustained with prayer. Historical revivals and awakenings were always preceded by the fervent cries

---

15   Encouragements to pray include Romans 8:26, 12:12, 15:30, I Corinthians 7:5, 11:4-13, 14:15, 2 Corinthians 1:11, Ephesians 6:18, Philippians 1:19, 4:6, Colossians 4:2-3, I Thess 5:17, 25, 2 Thessalonians 3:1, I Timothy 2:1, 8, Hebrews 13:18, James 5:13-18, I Peter 3:7,12, 4:7, I John 5:14-15, Jude 20. Prayer is used as an example in Romans 1:9, 10:1, 2 Corinthians 13:7, 13:9, Eph. 1:16, Phil 1:3-4, 9, Colossians 1:3,9, 4:12, I Thess. 1:2, 3:9-10, 2 Thess 1:11, I Timothy 5:5, 2 Timothy 1:3, Philemon 1:4, Hebrews 5:7, 3 John 1:2
16   I Thessalonians 5:17

of God's people to pour out His Spirit. Christianity has always been fueled by those who follow the way of Jesus and the apostles by prioritizing prayer.

The Practical Challenges of Prioritizing Prayer

Despite the overwhelming biblical evidence of the need to prioritize prayer, you have to come to grips with the reality of your calendar and daily habits. By now you know that you *should* pray first, but *how* do you find time to do so? I have found that if you really think something is important, then you intentionally make space for it to happen. You would definitely prioritize meeting an admired president or celebrity if they asked for an appointment.

What if you want to make time for God, but your calendar is full? The best solution is probably to wake up earlier. I am a night owl, so I hate to recommend this, but it's just the ideal time to pray. There's something about beginning your day with God that sets the tone for everything happening later. Mark 1:35 tells us Jesus woke up "very early in the morning" to pray. Other saints throughout church history have followed Jesus's example, sometimes in extravagant ways.

You may also need to stop doing some things so you can prioritize your relationship with the Lord. Humbly and honestly evaluate your life. Most people are too busy[17]. If you cannot find time for prayer, you have too much going on. If you simplify your schedule and reduce your commitments, your prayers may naturally blossom in the spaces and margins of your life.

With that said, modern research gives us some practical tips to help our brains and bodies cooperate with our hearts desire to make prioritizing prayer a habit in our lives. Here are a few suggestions that I have borrowed from author James Clear. If

---

17   May I suggest John Mark Comer's book *The Ruthless Elimination of Hurry*

you'd like to dive more deeply into the science of habits, you can check out his best-selling book *Atomic Habits*.

1. **Set a time.** Write it down. Put it on the calendar. Clear calls this an "implementation intention"[18].
2. **Pair your prayer time with another daily activity.** Clear calls this "habit stacking."[19] Do you get up and drink a cup of coffee every day? Have morning "Jesus and Java" time. Do you take a shower in the morning? Read a few Bible chapters before showering.
3. **Create a good environment for prayer.** Clear calls this "environment design"[20]. Jesus preferred mountains. The apostles prayed by a river. Find or create a good place that's conducive to prayer.
4. **Don't overcommit.** Clear suggests starting habits that are two minutes or less[21]. If you're not praying daily, start with two minutes every day. After a while, increase the time.
5. **Use accountability.** Clear calls this joining a "culture" where your new habit is encouraged and celebrated.[22] Find a friend whom you can text every day, asking each other about your prayer times.

These practical tips for building habits, combined with the New Testament call to prioritize prayer, will give you the faith and tools to put the presence of God at the center of your life. Everything flows from your relationship with the Lord. Give it time. Stay steady in faith. Follow the example of Jesus and put prayer first. Abide in Him and you will bear fruit.

---

18 https://jamesclear.com/implementation-intentions
19 https://jamesclear.com/habit-stacking
20 https://jamesclear.com/environment-design-organ-donation
21 https://jamesclear.com/how-to-stop-procrastinating
22 https://twitter.com/JamesClear/status/1220160115266945024

FOUR

Keys to Enjoyable Prayer

These first four chapters have been focused on laying the foundations of biblical prayer. We have clarified why we pray — the purpose of prayer is to cultivate a loving, personal relationship with God. We have identified to whom we pray —we approach God as our loving Father. We have highlighted when we are to pray — prayer should be first, because everything flows from intimacy with the Lord.

With these foundations in place, the upcoming chapters will look at how we should pray. I will share four important keys that will unlock greater joy in your relationship with God — combining worship and prayer, praying the Bible, hearing God's voice, and staying persistent.

Part Two: Keys to Enjoyable Prayer

WORSHIP: COMBINING MUSIC AND PRAYER

I remember exactly where I was sitting when I heard the first album by the band Sonicflood. I was in the corner office of my parents' house. I put the pink CD in the CD-ROM drive of the clunky, tan-colored 1990s desktop PC tower and cranked up the powered speakers.

I was enjoying the music when I suddenly realized that they were singing songs I had heard at church. The only difference was that it sounded... cool. My teenage mind was blown as I listened to Jeff Deyo belt out the chorus of a familiar Vineyard worship tune:

"*I want to know You*
I want to hear Your voice
I want to know You more
I want to touch You
I want to see Your face
I want to know You more..."

I had never heard worship music that sounded like Sonicflood. Up to that point, I mostly listened to Christian rock music that sang *about* God. DC Talk. Newsboys. Audio Adrenaline. Jars of Clay. This was the standard menu of late 90s CCM for a youth group kid. I would also go to church with my parents, and we would sing the less-enjoyable songs that were written *to* God. But I never listened to church music outside of Sunday mornings. Why would I do that? Church music wasn't cool. But then, sitting in a dilapidated office chair, I experienced a collision between the two worlds. Sonicflood was singing *to* God using modern pop-rock music.

What does this have to do with prayer? Musical worship was the gateway for me to experience true intimacy with God. God used songs to lead me into His presence. I inadvertently sang my prayers before I learned to speak them. I thought that prayer was boring, but I loved music. And God used this love for music to draw me to Himself.

Like most teenagers, my identity was deeply connected to my musical tastes. Music is not just something teenagers listen to; it is part of who they are as an individual. The importance of music in my life was heightened by the fact that I had started playing guitar when I was twelve years old. After my childhood dreams of being a professional baseball player shattered in the reality of a few competitive local little league seasons, I turned to music. I found that playing barre chords was easier for me than hitting a home run.

Our pastor, Joseph Sasser, started giving me private guitar lessons, and apparently I learned pretty quickly. Within a few months, I had written my first song. Pastor Joseph gave me prophetic words that God had called me to be a "psalmist" (whatever that meant), and he would always tell me that the only purpose of music was to worship and glorify God.

"A pastor has to say that," I thought. I kept bringing him my Third Day and Jars of Clay CDs so that he would teach me the Christian rock music. He kept trying to teach me church songs. I learned some of both, but I didn't care as much about the worship

WORSHIP: COMBINING MUSIC AND PRAYER

stuff. I wanted to learn guitar to be cool. Major League Baseball was no longer my goal. My new plan was to be a rock star.

I had been playing guitar for about three years when I heard that first Sonicflood album. Most of it was high-energy, but the last track was a simple acoustic version of Matt Redman's "Heart of Worship." The song was not nearly as exciting as the others, but something about it drew me in. I kept listening to the lyrics:

"When the music fades and all is stripped away…
I'll bring You more than a song
For a song in itself
Is not what You have required
You search much deeper within
through the way things appear
You're looking into my heart…"

The lyrics of these songs, coupled with words of truth from my pastor, landed like seeds in my heart. Something deeper than a desire to play music was happening. It would take a few years for these seeds to grow and bear fruit in my life, but God was already working.

Discovering Prayer Through Music

Fast forward a few years, and I began stepping into God's calling on my life as a worship leader. I shared in my book *David's Tabernacle* about the life-changing summer camp encounter I had with God right after graduating high school. God had touched my life, and I wanted others to experience that same love I had felt. We began a Friday night youth-oriented worship night called 6:22 where we would worship for hours, and students would experience God's life-changing presence and power. By that time, a lot of other "cool" worship music had gained traction. Along with Sonicflood, other modern worship bands such as Delirious,

Hillsong United, and Passion had emerged. Our 6:22 band played every energetic worship song we could find from any of these artists — and as loudly as possible.

God also dealt with my selfish desire to be a rock star in that season. My summer camp encounter had humbled me, set me free, and opened my heart to using my life and talents for God's glory instead of my own. I was still a young adult who was tempted by pride and self-promotion like anyone else, but over the next few years God cleared out the lingering thoughts of selfish ambition in my soul. By God's grace, I gradually released the idea of being a rock star and embraced God's call to ministry for my life.

However, if you had asked me about "prayer" I would have said that it was important, boring, and hard. The idea of "intercession" would be even more foreign. I loved Jesus. I loved music. But I would not have considered myself a prayerful person. Like many Christians, I felt guilty for not praying enough.

What I didn't realize is that I actually had a prayer life. The problem was that I did not understand the nature of prayer, so I thought prayer had to look a certain way to count before God. Many of the ways I experienced God involved music, so I called them "worship" instead of "prayer." I thought prayer required me to go somewhere quiet, close my eyes, clasp my hands, and just start talking to God for a period of time. I assumed that prayer ended when I stopped talking or opened my eyes. Yet in that season of my life, I was doing several things that I now realize were actually forms of prayer.

- I would put on a worship CD, crank up the stereo, and dance around the room (by "dance" I mean I would jump around and flail my arms) when no one was looking. Was I dancing a prayer?

- Other times I would sit down with my guitar and sing to Jesus. After singing a familiar song I might go "off script" for a while — singing from my heart to God in my own words. Sometimes these spontaneous moments would turn into songs. Was I singing my prayers?
- Before our Friday night worship gatherings, I would go out to the church with a pillow. I would put on some worship music, lie on the ground, and just rest to prepare my heart. Most of the time I was just "soaking" in God's presence and trying to hear His voice. Was my resting and listening also prayer?
- I had journals where I would write out my thoughts, struggles, frustrations, fears, and dreams. Sometimes I would address these journal entries to God. Was I writing my prayers?
- I had started reading my Bible more regularly. I tried to stick to an annual Bible reading plan. I skipped a lot of days, but I was still reading more than ever. Sometimes verses would stick out to me as I went through the daily passages. Was this God speaking to me? And was this part of prayer, too?

I believe it was all prayer. I had a narrow understanding of prayer that needed to be reshaped by the Word of God. I had some unbiblical religious mindsets that caused me to believe God wanted the activity of "prayer" rather than the truth that God wants intimacy with His children — and that there are a plethora of ways to experience that intimacy with Him. God was teaching me to pray. I just didn't recognize it. But by God's grace, I stumbled into some keys to enjoyable prayer that unlocked the door to intimacy with God. Music was the first key.

The Power of Music to Open Our Hearts

The Bible talks about singing over 200 times. What does it mean that God himself sings (Zephaniah 3:17)? Or that He designs His heavenly throne room with musical instruments (Revelation 5:8)? How did the stars sing at creation (Job 38:7)? How did David drive away demons with his harp (I Samuel 16:23)? Why did Elisha invite a minstrel before he would prophesy (2 Kings 3:15)? What does it mean that David taught his musicians to "prophesy" with their instruments (I Chronicles 25:1)? Can instruments speak (I Corinthians 14:7)? What was it about Samuel's band that made king Saul turn "into another man" (I Samuel 10:5-6)? What were the timbrels/tambourines in the garden of Eden (Ezekiel 28:13)?

Why did God create people (and some animals) to make musical notes and tones with their bodies? What exactly happens inside our brains when we combine language with melody? Why do kids learn better if you teach them with songs? Why do dementia patients remember more when they hear familiar songs? Why is music used for therapy? Why is music always used to build a strong culture and community? Why does singing relieve stress and improve one's immune system?

I think it is because God likes music. There is something about music that allows you to experience God's presence in a profound way. Perhaps it's because the very characteristics of music — the beauty, the order, the creativity, the rhythm, the words, the emotions — reflects the very nature of God Himself. God is musical, and musical worship is a gift from Him to help us pray with joy and experience His love. Music provides an enjoyable and natural way for you to open your heart and emotions to the power and presence of God in your life.

The Joy of God's Presence in Worship

I cannot talk about music in the Bible without talking about praise. Praise is the most common use of music in Scriptures. The Psalms encourage praising God with singing, shouting, dancing, bowing down, lifting hands, and playing musical instruments. By far, the most common way to praise God in Scripture is through singing.

Praise is actually a type of prayer. Jesus begins and ends the Lord's prayer with praise: *"Our Father in heaven, hallowed be Your name.... Yours is the kingdom and the power and the glory forever"*[1]. I urge you to be intentional in starting and ending your prayer times with thanking and praising God for who He is and what He has done. You can speak or sing these prayers, but they should be expressed verbally. Consider using music. Musical praise and worship in prayer will set your heart on the Lord, usher you into His presence, and ultimately make your time of prayer much more enjoyable. If you're not a trained musician, you can simply put on some anointed worship music and sing along.

The Bible teaches that we enter God's presence with thanksgiving and praise[2] and that He is enthroned on our praises[3]. So when Jesus encourages us to start our prayers with praise and worship, He is not primarily giving us a prayer formula; He is inviting us into His presence. By teaching us to pray with praise, He is showing us the kind of prayer that God desires. He wants intimate, worshipful prayer. He longs for His people to draw near to His heart, worship Him, and be with Him where He is.

This invitation to presence-centered prayer is an invitation to enjoyable prayer. Remember God's promise in Isaiah 56:7 that we

---

1   Matthew 6:9, 13 [NKJV]
2   See Psalm 100:4
3   Psalm 22:3

would be joyful in the house of prayer? This verse asks *how* we can find joy in the place of prayer. I believe Psalm 16:11 gives us a key.

> *In your presence there is fullness of joy; at your right hand are pleasures forevermore.*

There is joy in the house of prayer because it is filled with the manifest presence of God. God Himself brings delight, pleasure, satisfaction, beauty, rest, and glory. In God's presence there is fullness of joy, and we enter God's presence with praise. Therefore enjoyable prayer should be worship-based prayer.

Harps & Bowls

Prayer and worship flow together seamlessly in heaven and on earth. Thanksgiving, praise, prayer, and intercession are all about alignment and agreement with God. Praise is agreement with who God is, and prayer is agreement with what God wants to do. In fact, we see this reality in the apostle John's scene of the heavenly throne room.

While the four living creatures in heaven cry out "Holy, holy, holy" incessantly, there are twenty-four elders also gathered around the throne of God. In Revelation 5:8 we see that these elders are holding two items — harps and bowls. The harps are musical instruments of praise and worship to God. The bowls are full of incense which John tells us are the prayers of the saints. Songs of worship and prayers of intercession are mingled together and offered to God as a unified sacrifice to Jesus in heaven.

> *And when he had taken the scroll, the four living creatures and the twenty-four elders fell down before the Lamb, each holding a harp, and golden bowls full of incense, which are the prayers of the saints. Revelation 5:8*

In the kingdom of God, musical worship and prayer go hand in hand. Intimacy and intercession are two sides of the same coin. If we pursue God's heart and presence with worshipful hearts, lives, and songs, we will find ourselves caught up into a life of prayer that is deeper and more enjoyable that we could ever imagine. We will find ourselves lost in a flow of joyful thanksgiving, praise, and intercession. We will realize our simple words, songs, and actions can touch God's heart and change the course of history.

When Jesus taught us to "hallow" the name of the Lord, He was inviting us into heavenly joy. To hallow means to recognize something as holy or sacred, and the "name" of the Lord is His nature and person. To pray in the way of Jesus is to join with the heavenly song around the throne of God where the angels sing "holy, holy, holy" day and night. As we hallow His name, we align with heaven and join their praise, and an inexplicable spiritual exchange takes place. A bit more heaven comes to earth, and we are changed forever.

How to Combine Music and Prayer

You may be wondering how to combine musical worship and prayer in a practical way. Here are a few suggestions.

1. **Begin and End with Praise.** As I mentioned earlier, a great first step is to simply begin and end your personal prayer times with thanksgiving and praise. Bookending your time with God in this way will help you keep it about Him and not just the needs and requests you bring to Him.
2. **Sing Your Prayers.** I encourage you to experiment with singing your prayers. This is very unusual and unfamiliar for most people, but it was not uncommon in Hebrew culture. Much of the Bible was originally sung, including

praise, prayers, and prophecies. They even sang the law of God[4].

3. **Live Stream a Prayer Room.** There are prayer rooms that live stream their prayer meetings where they combine musical praise, prayer, worship, and intercession. You can watch how they flow together and sing along with them as they sing biblical prayers to God[5]. If possible, try to find a similar prayer room near you and visit it in person.

4. **Sing the Bible & Sing in Tongues.** As we'll discuss in subsequent chapters, you can sing through Scriptures as a way to pray and interact with the Lord. You can also sing in tongues. The Bible encourages many enjoyable and creative ways to engage with God.

5. **Worship-Based Prayer Meetings.** For those leading prayer meetings, I can provide some additional resources for you about how to combine musical worship and prayer with teams as you lead and host corporate prayer gatherings. Please visit enjoyingprayer.com for more.

---

4   See Psalm 119:54 for example
5   For example, check out the prayer room videos from International House of Prayer in Kansas City, Upperroom Church in Dallas, or Radiant Church in Kalamazoo.

SCRIPTURE: THE LANGUAGE OF PRAYER

Our family has a hilarious childhood video of my brother and me on his birthday. My brother Mark was maybe four years old, and I was around seven. One of his gifts was a children's Bible. As you watch him open it on the grainy VHS tape, you can hear my very southern, high-pitched voice declare "Mark, that is the best present you could get!" A few moments later, you see me sitting on the floor with my brother's new children's Bible, reading it as loudly as possible to the room.

My younger brother, however, was not impressed. While I was reading the story, Mark was acting like a hyperactive four-year-old who probably just had too much cake. He was climbing every piece of furniture, jumping off the couch, doing backflips off the recliner, somersaulting on the floor, and ignoring me with all his might. He was oblivious to me, and I was oblivious to him. At seven years old, I was so proud of being able to read "the best present you could get" to my little brother that I didn't even notice what was going on around me. With dogged first-born determination, I kept my head down and powered through the story of Adam and Eve. Mark, meanwhile, continued to flail carelessly around the room, only pausing briefly to offer a few bored sighs. The juxtaposition of the video is quite amusing, and our family references it regularly when we get together on holidays.

"The best present ever." Even from a young age, I always seemed to have a high value for Scripture. I knew instinctively that a Bible was a valuable gift; and it is. The unparalleled collection of sixty-six books is a supernatural work of the Spirit. The Bible is the best-selling book of all time, and rightfully so. It is God's Word to us. And while the Holy Spirit can speak to us subjectively, the Scriptures are God's objective Word to His people, by which all other words are judged. The Bible is our source of understanding God's nature, His plan, and His heart. The Bible is God's infallible Word. It stands alone above every other Christian book as the authority for Christians.

> *All Scripture is breathed out by God and profitable for teaching, for reproof, for correction, and for training in righteousness. 2 Timothy 3:16*

The Bible As A Doorway Relationship with God

When read rightly, the Bible is a gateway into intimate relationship with the Lord. The Scriptures themselves show us that the words on the page are not an end to themselves, but are meant to help us connect to God. It is possible to approach the Bible in a way that misses God. The Scriptures are not the source of life but they point us to the Source of life. This is what Jesus himself said:

> *You search the Scriptures because you think that in them you have eternal life; and it is they that bear witness about me. John 5:39*

The Bible is holy, but the Bible is not God — no more than a love note from my wife could ever replace my wife. Obviously the

SCRIPTURE: THE LANGUAGE OF PRAYER

Scriptures are much more profound than a "love note from God," but my point still stands. The letter kills, but the Spirit gives life.[1] Studying the Bible apart from a relationship with God is fruitless.

The Word of God is designed to be a place of encounter with His presence. Its purpose is to facilitate loving interaction with the Lord, and therefore it is inseparable from prayer. I have found over the years that the Bible is one of the primary tools that helps me have a conversational, revelatory, and enjoyable prayer life. It is truly magnificent! And we do not honor it enough.

There is a powerful video that went viral of Christians in an underground church receiving their own Bibles for the first time. They are weeping and rejoicing, clutching the books as if they were gold, and falling to their knees with grateful hearts of worship. It is convicting. Do I value God's word like they do? Sitting here in my office as I write this chapter, I stopped and counted twelve different copies of the Bible on my bookshelf behind me. I have an app on my phone where I can freely access the Bible anytime in dozens of languages and translations. The convenience and access we have to the Scriptures in the western world can desensitize us to the treasure that God has provided for us.

Some of the most life-changing and joyous encounters with God in my life happened as I sat with the Bible open on my lap in front me. The words in the Bible have provided comfort, wisdom, clarity, excitement, purpose, identity, insight, peace, refreshing, healing, and conviction. God's Word is powerful! The Bible has also given me language, direction, and prophetic insight about how to pray.

Don't just pray *and* read the Bible. *Pray the Bible*. Read the Bible prayerfully and pray biblically. When you open the book, let it be

---

[1] 2 Corinthians 3:6

the start of a conversation with the Author. And when you pray, always grab your Bible. Below I list five reasons to pray the Bible. Then I will share some practical tools about how to integrate this in your life.

Five Reasons to Pray the Bible

1. **The Bible Models Praying the Bible.** Prayers are recycled many times in Scripture. For instance, King David gave a song to the singers in I Chronicles 16 that was also recorded in Psalm 105 that was also prayed in Isaiah 12. Jesus prayed the Psalms, and even quoted Psalm 22:1 while hanging on the cross. The apostle Paul instructs the New Testament church to sing/pray the word of God in Colossians 3:16.

2. **There is Power in God's Word.** You can pray from your own heart with your own words, but you also need to pray in agreement with God. Coming into alignment with God's Word has power and will give you confidence. Hebrews 4:12 says *"For the word of God is living and active, sharper than any two-edged sword, piercing to the division of soul and of spirit..."* and Isaiah 55:11 says *"So shall my word be that goes out from my mouth; it shall not return to me empty, but it shall accomplish that which I purpose..."*

3. **Praying the Bible grounds our prayers theologically.** I have heard quite a few prayers spoken that were downright unbiblical. Forcing yourself to pray from the Scriptures helps you orient your prayers in the truth of God's Word. Then you will not ask for what you want, but for what God wants.

4. **Praying the Bible gives language.** Sometimes you may not know what to pray or how to pray. When you pray from the Bible you always have something to say. If you're

having a bad day or your mind is scattered, you can just flip open your Bible and speak God's Word back to Him. You will always have language for our prayers.

5. **Praying the Bible unites the Church.** This is especially helpful when praying with Christians from multiple churches or denominations. All Christians agree on the authority of God's Word, and praying Bible prayers gives us common ground from which to cry out to God together.

The Recipe for Prayerful Bible Meditation

How do we "pray the Bible"? What does this look like practically? I offer a few suggestions of practices that have been helpful to me over the years. The important thing is that you *interact with God through His Word.* The goal is never to plod religiously through a certain prayer strategy or formula; the goal is to cultivate a loving relationship with the Lord.

There are many ways to do this. As you read the bible, pause and praise Him for his attributes and activity. I love to note the adjectives and verbs that describe God's actions and nature. What is He like? What is He doing? Why is He doing it? Go slow. Praise Him for His actions and His motives. Thank Him for every unconditional promise. Ask God to fulfill every prophecy. Turn your Bible reading into intercession. As you gain insights into God's purposes, come into agreement with His Word by asking Him to do what His Word says is in His heart to do. Ask questions about things that stick out to you or confuse you. Pause. Allow the Holy Spirit to give you understanding. Write down what comes to mind. Keep asking. Keep listening.

One of the tools that has helped many people to pray God's Word is an approach to biblical meditation developed by Kirk

Bennett. He uses a simple five-step approach to interacting with Scripture:

Read it.

Write it.

Say it.

Sing it.

Pray it.

Kirk calls this the recipe (RWSSP) for biblical meditation[2]. These five ways of engaging Scripture will open your heart to truth in a fresh way and lead you into encounters with God through the Bible. Most people primarily interact with the Bible through reading. This is the equivalent of taking a bite of food and immediately swallowing. Taking the time to write, say, sing, and pray the Scriptures is a way to "chew" God's word. It becomes more digestible for your heart and soul.

These steps seem so simple, but it is transformative to take the extra time to meditate on Scripture in these ways. Writing, speaking, and singing all engage your brain in different ways, and help the Word of God settle into your heart and mind. Praying the Bible helps lead you into deeper revelation of what God really says.

The Word of God is alive and active. It is powerful and deep, with layers of revelation, patterns, understanding, wisdom, and insights. As you go deeper with God through His Word, you should find it easier to spend long periods of time meditating on one verse or even one phrase from a verse. There are libraries of understanding packed away in each word that God has intentionally written for us in the Bible. Writing, praying, and

---

[2] We could spend more time on each step of the RWSSP method of Bible meditation, but for those who want to learn more, I would suggest getting a copy of Kirk's Bible meditation manual on Kirk's website at 7thunders.org.

singing Scripture can provide hours and hours of time with the Lord that is revelatory and life-changing.

One of the easiest sections of the Bible from which to pray is the book of Psalms. It is a book of prayer, worship, poetry, and prophecy that has been an integral part of Christian worship for all of church history. Its devotional nature makes it simple to use as a launchpad for prayer and worship. The raw and honest nature of many of the psalms makes the prayers feel relatable and human. Yet at the same time, many of the psalms call you higher. They reveal aspects of God's character that encourage, surprise, and excite you. They urge you to look to God amid challenges, suffering, and hardships. The Psalms are a collision of the transcendent and the imminent. Especially in times of devotional prayer, the book of Psalms is an invaluable resource for connecting to God through His Word.

The Importance of Repetition and Revelation

When we speak of meditating on Scripture, we inevitably run into the issue of repetition. If you take the time to read, write, say, sing, and pray the Bible, then you find yourself saying the same phrases over and over again. Some people push back against repetitive approaches to prayer because of Jesus' instructions in Matthew 6 about avoiding vain repetition. We should heed the warning of Jesus, but I want to argue that not all repetition is bad. In fact, I would argue that repetition is vital for the Word of God to take root in our hearts the way God desires.

The Bible encourages day and night meditation on its contents. Psalm 1:2 advises God's people to delight in His law and meditate on it "day and night" to avoid wickedness and be fruitful. This chapter, and others such as Psalm 119[3] clearly show that meditation was a central tenant to the worship and prayer that

---

3   See verses like Psalm 119:97-98 or verse 148

King David established.[4] The original Hebrew words translated into "meditate" in these verses mean exactly what you would expect. They mean to muse or study or imagine or mutter. In other words, thinking and speaking about something repetitively is exactly what God is commanding us to do with His word.

The Bible does not condemn the practice of praying God's Word over and over. It endorses it. In fact, in other teachings on prayer Jesus encourages persistence[5]. If other passages of Scripture seem to encourage repetition, persistent prayer, and Bible meditation, then we have to reexamine Jesus' warning against vain repetition. God is not contradicting Himself. Let's look at the passage.

> And when you pray, do not use <u>vain repetitions</u> as the heathen do. For they think that they will be heard for their many words. Therefore do not be like them. For your Father knows the things you have need of before you ask Him.
> Matthew 6:7-8 [NKJV]

Jesus condemned *vain* repetition, but not all repetition is wrong. The important word here is "vain." The context of this verse shows that Jesus was condemning the hypocrisy and religiosity of the Pharisees who were praying publicly and repetitively in order to impress others. A few verses earlier Jesus described them praying "standing in the synagogues and on the corners of the streets".

The issue was not repetition; the issue was their hearts. They were not trying to commune with God and cultivate an intimate relationship with their Father. They were self-righteously performing their ritualistic prayers to be seen by men. The ESV translation renders "vain repetition" as "empty phrases." They

---

[4] At that time, the Torah, or "the law" (the first five books of the Bible) was the only Scripture they had to meditate on. Now that we have the totality of Scripture, how much more should we meditate on God's Word!

[5] See Luke 11:9-13, 18:1-8

were saying a lot of words, but they were not truly praying. It was their self-centered religiosity that was rebuked, not the fact that they repeated themselves.

Praying God's Word with a sincere heart of love is not using "empty phrases." Quite the contrary. It is powerful. Repetition in prayer can help lead us into revelation, if our hearts truly desire to know God more. Do not be afraid of offending Jesus by repeating your prayers, singing Bible phrases over and over or spending extended time meditating on His Word. If your heart is to really know and love God more, then these things are pure and biblical ways to pray.

Apostolic Prayers

One final tool I encourage you to consider as you're praying the Bible is to pray the apostolic prayers. Apostolic prayers is a term for New Testament prayers that we have recorded from Jesus,[6] Paul, Peter, and John. It is amazing that we can borrow the language and themes of the prayers of these saints and pray them as our own. I have found that the apostolic prayers are especially helpful in my intercession. These verses are my go-to source of direction regarding how I pray for my family, friends, church, city, and nation.

I credit Mike Bickle for exposing me and many others to these passages of Scripture and the power of using them in our prayer lives[7]. I have gleaned heavily from his insights regarding the nature of these prayers and some of the best ways to use them. I have included a list of some apostolic prayers as a free download at enjoyingprayer.com. Some of my favorites include the apostle Paul's prayers in Ephesians,[8] the Lord's Prayer, and Jesus's high priestly prayer in John 17. There are many others.

---

6   Jesus is also called an apostle in Hebrews 3:1, so his prayers are included.
7   See chapter nine of Bickle's book *Growing in Prayer* for more.
8   Ephesians 1:17-19 and 3:16-19

These are the three basic ways I pray through the apostolic prayers:
1. Say the phrases back to God exactly as they are written.
2. Use my own language to express the same idea to the Lord.
3. Develop the broad theme of the passage with extended prayers and other verses as the Holy Spirit leads.

As I have said many times in this chapter, there is power in praying God's Word. We know for certain that the prayers uttered by the original apostles and recorded in the canon of Scripture reflect what God really wants. So you can pray these Bible passages with confidence knowing that these are prayers that God wills to answer. You do not have to discern if God wants his kingdom to come to earth[9] — you can simply pray for it. You do not need a prompting from the Spirit before you pray for God to reveal His love — you know He wants to do it. When you don't know what to pray, you can simply open your Bible and speak His Word back to Him with assurance that He will answer.

However, one thing I discovered while initially trying to pray through these apostolic prayers is that I had very little understanding of what they were even talking about. I encourage you to pause right now and read Paul's prayer in Ephesians 1:17-19. Be honest. How much of what he said do you comprehend? It's quite a prayer! And as I started looking at these apostolic prayers years ago, so many of the phrases were foreign to me. What is the spirit of wisdom and revelation? What is the hope of His calling? What does it mean that we would be with Jesus where He is? What does it mean to be filled with the fullness of God?

My desire to align my prayers with the Word of God exposed the fact that many of my thoughts were not oriented to the same

---

9   Matthew 6:10

ideas or language of the Bible. I needed a paradigm shift. I was in the habit of praying phrases I had learned in American Christian subculture or simply asking God to "bless" people (whatever that means). I was severely disconnected from the desires that the apostles expressed in their prayers for the church. This meant that to pray biblically, I had to take time to learn what exactly was important to God. What kind of things should we be praying about? My default prayers were in stark contrast to those of the New Testament.

This is where these apostolic prayers are so helpful. They align us to the will of God. The apostolic prayers not only gave me language from which to pray, but that have reformed my understanding of God's purposes for humanity. They have reoriented my understanding about what is really important to the Lord. Much of what I thought God wanted was really what I wanted. I realized that much of what I prayed for was not that high on God's priority list. One of the benefits of praying the apostolic prayers, even in an intercessory way, has been that I have been transformed by them. Intercessors will have their minds renewed to be more like Christ as they pray these Scripture passages.

The apostolic prayers, like the entire Bible, are an incredible resource that we can utilize to interact with God in a way that cultivates love in our hearts, makes us more like Him, and releases His power into the earth. God's Word is powerful. It gives us faith and confidence in who He is and what He wants to do. Taking the time to meditate on Scripture through reading, writing, saying, singing, and praying it brings revelation and transformation. It is one of the most important keys to experiencing enjoyable prayer.

LISTENING: HEARING GOD'S VOICE IN PRAYER

As I sit down to write this chapter, my throat is extremely sore. I have been trying to rest my voice all day and speak as little as possible. Yet I am struggling with feeling like I haven't prayed today. I am prone to think about prayer as *talking* to God, but what happens when I can't speak? Is there still a way to pray? Can I commune with God beyond my own voice?

My sore throat has been a timely reminder of a deeper fellowship in prayer that God desires. There is a way to become aware of His presence in stillness and silence. There is a way to hear His voice through His Word and by His Spirit. There are creative ways to engage with the Lord through journaling, writing, and creative arts. None of these involve talking to God, per se. But they can all be an expression of prayer.

In fact, you can easily become religious in your approach to prayer and assume that you have really interacted with God when, in reality, you have only spoken words to God. There is a difference. You can recite prayers and never really touch the heart of God. Jesus said in Matthew 15:8:

> "This people honors me with their lips, but their heart is far from me."

You need more than religious prayer. You need to really know God. You need your heart to be close to his. You need to experience His presence intimately and personally. As I have said, prayer is not talking *to* God; it is talking *with* God. This seems like a great sentiment, but the problem is that it is much easier for most people to talk to God than to hear His voice. For prayer to be relational you have to be able to flow in conversation with the Lord. But how does God speak? And how do you know if it's really His voice, rather than your own imagination or the voice of the enemy trying to deceive you?

God Is Speaking

I believe God speaks directly to people. Jesus made that very clear in John 10:27 when He said, "My sheep hear My voice, and I know them, and they follow Me." Throughout the Bible, you see God speaking to His people in direct ways. God wants to lead you in a personal way, like the Good Shepherd that He is. If God is speaking to His people, then the true struggle is not with *hearing* God's voice, but with *discerning* God's voice. He is speaking to you; you are hearing Him; you just may not realize it sometimes.

Understanding the way that God tends to speak to you can help you grow in your discernment of the voice of the Lord in your life. As you begin to notice Him speaking to you, your love for Him will grow exponentially. Prayer will begin to seem like friendship. Obedience will start feeling like partnership. Bible reading will turn into an adventure. Your life will become a journey that you take with God as His friend, rather than an obligation to please Him as HIs servant.

Hearing God in The Bible

The primary way God speaks is through the Scriptures. The Bible is God's word, and is vital in learning to cultivate a relationship with Him. Every verse is inspired by the Holy

Spirit. It is divine, and it provides a bedrock of truth to build your life upon. God will never speak in a way that contradicts Himself, which means He will never contradict His written word in Scripture. 2 Timothy 3:16 says:

> Scripture is given by inspiration of God, and is profitable for doctrine, for reproof, for correction, for instruction in righteousness.

As you read the Bible, you can hear God's voice. Have you ever had a certain verse or passage jump out at you as you read? That is the voice of God. That is the Holy Spirit illuminating specific truth to you. All of the Bible is God's word and is valuable; however, sometimes the "spirit of revelation" "opens the eyes of our heart"[1] to see and understand in ways we have never experienced.

I have also found that sometimes the Holy Spirit will randomly bring a Bible verse to mind throughout the day. This is another way He speaks. He does this to encourage you, remind you of truth, or to give you something you can share with others. Jesus promised His disciples that the Holy Spirit would help remind them of what He had already spoken to them. In John 14:26 He says:

> But the Helper, the Holy Spirit, whom the Father will send in my name, he will teach you all things and bring to your remembrance all that I have said to you.

The reminders from the Holy Spirit can only happen as you regularly fill your heart and mind with Scripture. Reading the Bible is the starting point for hearing God speak.

I am old enough to remember when phones would not show a caller ID. The phone would ring, and you picked up the receiver

---

[1] Ephesians 1:17-18

and said "Hello?" to find out who was on the other line. If you were calling someone you did not know well, your response would be to first introduce yourself to the person who just answered on the other end of the line. However, if you knew the caller really well, no introductions were necessary. If a parent called a child or a husband called a wife, the initial "Hello?" would be followed by a "Hey! What's up?" from the other person. They immediately recognized the caller's voice because of the tone and inflection they heard.

What is my point? Reading the Bible is a way to learn the *tone* of God's voice. The more I know about the God of the Bible, the more I can recognize Him when He's interacting with me or speaking to me in other ways. By studying God's written Word, I grow in understanding His nature, so discerning His voice becomes more natural. When a still, small voice speaks to us. we can know it's God because we have heard that tone before.

Silence and Solitude

Perhaps one of the reasons that many still struggle to hear God's voice is because our lives are so filled with noise. Every moment of the day is filled with screens flashing, notifications buzzing, music playing and people wanting our attention. Many people turn on their phones as soon as they wake up, only to be bombarded with the latest news, text messages, and social media updates. We find ourselves so overstimulated that we do not even know how to pause and be still.

The Scriptures invite you to draw away to God in stillness and solitude to commune with Him and hear His voice. Psalm 46:10 says "Be still, and know that I am God." When the prophet Elijah was overcome with depression after battling with Jezebel, he hid in a cave, and God came to speak to him. There was a great wind, a strong earthquake, and a terrifying fire. Elijah waited safely in the cave, while the noise and chaos raged around him — similar to the noise and chaos of our lives, filled with technological stimulation and overscheduled calendars. Yet God was not in the big, loud, exciting moments; after the wind, earthquake, and fire subsided, Elijah heard God speak. What he heard was not a thundering voice from heaven but a "low whisper" or a "still, small voice."[2]

Many say they want to hear from God, but who is regularly taking the time to stop and listen? In order to hear from God clearly, you need to press in and wait for the still small voice of the Holy Spirit. Your mind may race. You may get distracted. You may want to pick up your phone or turn on the TV. But if you wait for the Lord, there is a treasure to be found after everything in your soul settles. Just as someone who is blind can develop an acute sense of hearing or smelling, I believe you can amplify God's voice in your heart as you slow down, get quiet, and disconnect from the whirlwind of activity.

The Bible commands us to wait on the Lord. This is not just an encouragement to be patient regarding God's promises, but it is an invitation to spend time with Him in patient silence and solitude. Just as a waiter "waits" on a table, you position yourself before God and wait for Him to speak. Waiting is not a passive position, but an active thoughtfulness that allows you to pay attention to God. This requires intentionality. In our day and time, every phone app, marketing guru and big tech corporation is researching the best way to get and keep your attention. Attention is a precious commodity, and Jesus is worthy of it. Solitude is a way to tell God that His voice is more important than all the other voices vying for your time and focus. Henri Nouwen says:

> "We enter into solitude first of all to meet our Lord and to be with him and him alone. Our primary task in solitude,

---

[2] I Kings 19:12

> *therefore, is not to pay undue attention to the many faces which assail us, but to keep the eyes of our mind and heart on him who is our divine savior."* [3]

The way you practice stillness may vary. I find it helpful to literally sit down with no sound, stare at the ground (or close my eyes, if I'm not too tired), and try to focus my thoughts on Jesus. I will usually set a timer for how long I want to wait and listen. I inevitably get distracted and have to constantly reorient my mind towards the Lord. Sometimes it helps me focus to imagine Jesus on the cross. Sometimes I envision the Father running towards me with open arms and a smile on His face, like the story of the prodigal son. Sometimes I will envision Him sitting right beside me on the couch, and we just sit together, without any pressure to say or do anything.

Sometimes God speaks clearly in those moments, and sometimes He does not. But it is always communion with Him. As I wait in silence and solitude, my awareness of His presence grows stronger and stronger. I take deep breaths — sometimes involuntarily. As the noise begins to fade and my mind begins to settle, I enter into a deep and sweet peace. This is prayer.

Jesus himself practiced solitude while on the earth. Mark 1:35 says:

> *And rising very early in the morning, while it was still dark, he departed and went out to a desolate place, and there he prayed.*

I would love to discover exactly what Jesus did in the desolate places when He got alone with the Father, but I do not think the specifics matter a lot. You do not have to practice silence and solitude the same way I do. Many people are more kinesthetic,

---

[3] *The Way of the Heart*, pg 20

and like to take walks, pace, or move around in some way as they wait on the Lord. The key is to disconnect from the ongoing noise of life and settle yourself in a way that you can tune into what's happening in your own soul, where the Holy Spirit abides. Often we cover up our own feelings and the voice of God by activity and overstimulation. If we can slow down, tune in, and be patient, we will find that the voice of God begins to "bubble up" inside of us through silence and solitude.

Hearing God Through Impressions

The Bible is God's *Word*, but it does not replace God's *voice*. In fact, when I read the Bible, I see clearly that God wants to speak to me in a direct and personal way. Some people falsely promote the idea that God does not speak to us anymore because we now have the canon of Scripture. Yet God's Word says that Jesus is the same yesterday, today, and forever[4]. He has spoken throughout history, and He continues to speak now. Why would Jesus bring us into a new covenant, fill us with His Spirit, and then cease communicating with us?

This raises the question, what does God's voice sound like? When God speaks to you, His voice is usually not audible. It is not typically a sound you will hear from outside you that comes to your ears. As a Christian, God's Spirit dwells inside you, so most of the time God's voice seems internal rather than external.

I believe God can speak audibly, though I have not had that experience. Those that have heard God audibly say that it is relatively rare and quite a jolting experience. I was with a man once as he heard (what he claims was) God's audible voice, and he immediately began weeping uncontrollably.

I believe that the most common way God speaks is through impressions. Impressions are simply thoughts that come to our

---

4   Hebrews 13:8

mind from God. It can feel more like having an idea than hearing a voice. But this is a primary way you can hear God's voice through the Holy Spirit. Mark Virkler says:

> "Recognize God's voice as spontaneous thoughts which light upon your mind."[5]

I have found this quote from Mark Virkler to be the most accurate definition I can find for the way God has spoken to me over the more than twenty years of having a relationship with Him. God's voice comes as "spontaneous thoughts which light upon your mind" that carry the tone of God's voice that we know from Scripture.

Sometimes impressions are more like feelings. Sometimes impressions are specific words or phrases that come to mind. Sometimes impressions come as vague or specific ideas. Sometimes impressions come as still or moving images in our imagination.

One way we notice that a thought or idea could be from the Holy Spirit is that it is spontaneous. Most people think linearly. One idea leads to a related idea which leads to a related idea, etc. But when God speaks, it tends to interrupt our existing train of thought. God's voice "breaks in" to our mind and reveals truth. If you have a random thought or idea, especially during times of worship and prayer, do not dismiss it. It could be the Lord speaking to you.

As you act based on the impressions God gives you, you will grow in your discernment. You may believe God has spoken something to you, so you take a step of faith based on what you heard. What you will find is that God will confirm what He has spoken to you with grace, joy, and peace. It does not mean that

---

[5] *4 Keys to Hearing God's Voice* by Mark Virkler

you will always want to hear what God is saying, but deep in your heart you will know that it is just what you need.

The longer you walk with God, stopping to listen and obey His voice, the clearer you'll be able to distinguish the voice of the Lord from your own thoughts or the whispers of the enemy. Your confidence will grow as you not only listen to God's Word, but respond with faith and obedience to what He is speaking to you.

Dreams and Visions

Receiving dreams and visions from God is a powerful way to hear from Him. The saying goes that a picture is worth a thousand words. Sometimes seeing something from God is even more impactful or descriptive than hearing from God with language. In Acts 2 the apostle Peter quotes the prophet Joel who declared that "young men shall see visions, and your old men shall dream dreams"[6].

Dreams and visions occurred throughout the Bible. Jacob, Joseph, Solomon, Daniel, Ezekiel and many other Old Testament characters heard from God through dreams in the night or visions in the day. Peter, Paul, Cornelius, John and others in the New Testament encountered God through dreams and visions.

Visions from God may be still pictures or animated "movies" in your imagination. They could flash into your mind briefly or last for a while. They may or may not include sounds. Visions may appear while your eyes are closed in prayer or it may feel like you "black out" as you receive a vision. Or your eyes may remain open while the vision is superimposed upon what your eyes are physically seeing. Dreams are like visions, but they obviously happen while one is asleep.

Just like impressions, many visions from God could be wrongly construed as one's own thoughts or ideas. Many people see things

---

6   Acts 2:17

in their imaginations or dreams and do not realize that God could be speaking to them visually. If you are in a time of prayer or worship and you have spontaneous images floating through your imagination that do not contradict the Bible's teaching, they probably are from God!

God frequently speaks visually to some people, depending on their particular spiritual gifts. Also, in my experience, there are seasons where God seems to ramp up the incidence of dreams and visions in one's life, particularly after a season of fasting.

The Subjectivity of Hearing God's Voice

With impressions, dreams and visions, God never says something that is not true, but it is very possible for us to misinterpret what He is saying. I strongly discourage you from stating over-confidently that God told you to do something. It is usually wiser to say "I think God said…" rather than "God definitely said…". The reason is that hearing and discerning God's voice is subjective. God's word in the Bible is objective truth, but our ability to hear the Holy Spirit can get distorted.

The issue is not the Speaker but the listener. Sometimes we think we have heard God, but we have not. Sometimes we hear God, but we put our own interpretation and spin on what He said. This doesn't mean that we should not seek to hear God or share what He's speaking. But it does mean that we should do so humbly while accepting the possibility that we could make mistakes. That is why I suggest you usually present what God has spoken to you by saying "I think God said."

Another way to avoid misspeaking on behalf of God is to discern the Lord's voice in the context of wise counsel. Being in community with other Spirit-filled believers who are knowledgeable of God's Word can help you get clarity as you seek to hear God speak. Proverbs 11:14 advises us:

LISTENING: HEARING GOD'S VOICE IN PRAYER

> *Where there is no guidance, a people falls, but in an abundance of counselors there is safety.*

As you are inviting others into your discernment journey, it is important that your counsel be wise counsel. Proverbs uses this term in reference to those who are discerning whether or not they should go to war.[7] By wise counsel, I do not necessarily mean those who are intelligent, but those who are more mature in the Lord and have a history with hearing God's voice accurately. A pastor or a spiritual mentor is a great place to start. If you are married to a believing spouse, then God will use your spouse as a source of discernment for you. If you think you have heard from God, but your pastor and wife disagree, then I can almost guarantee that you have been mistaken! As you learn and grow to hear from God, you should humbly heed the wisdom and counsel of mature saints that God has placed in your life.

You can learn to hear God's voice more clearly by slowing down your life, staying saturated in Scripture, and rooting yourself in a healthy community. This will allow you to pray relationally and joyfully by the Holy Spirit. Prayer is always more fun when it is interactive and conversational. Tuning into the voice of the Lord will lead you into the deep joy of friendship with God in prayer.

---

[7] Proverbs 20:18, 24:16

EIGHT

PERSISTENCE: STAYING FAITHFUL IN PRAYER

My wife and I once got to sit and chat with a faithful intercessor in our town named Nancy. She had befriended my mom when we first moved to Greenville when I was a little boy. Nancy mentored many young girls in their faith, and she was one of those legendary prayer warriors who had been faithful to Jesus for decades. Even into her eighties and nineties, she was always expectant for the new things that God was about to do.

We sat in her back sunroom and talked for a while. I wanted to ask her how she stayed zealous in prayer and intercession for decades. I had my notepad ready for a list of prayer "hacks" or best practices. I thought I might be able to even turn her wisdom into a blog post or a podcast episode. So, I asked her, and after thinking for a moment, she simply responded, "He won't let me go."

I put my notepad away. It was so simple and yet so profound! She had a revelation that it was not her own perseverance that sustained her; it was God's faithfulness towards her that allowed her to stay steady for decades. This totally shifted my paradigm about what it meant to be faithful and persistent in prayer.

Our faith is not a hopeful attitude that we muster up in our own strength. It is a deep trust in God. He is the faithful One, and we believe in Him. We lean into Him. We are empowered by His faithfulness to be faithful, even though none of us are perfect in our pursuit. But because our persistence in prayer is dependent on God, not us, we have hope. It is God who does it by His grace as we believe in Him and His Word.

God's Word Gives Us Faith to Pray

This deep, trusting faith is vital if you are going to have a long-lasting life of prayer and an enjoyable relationship with God. One reason the Bible is so powerful is because it gives you the revelation of God that establishes and fuels your faith. Romans 10:17 says,

> *So faith comes from hearing, and hearing through the word of Christ.*

Faith is believing and trusting in what God has spoken. It is not just mental ascent to facts or data; it is relational trust that requires acting as if you truly believe what has been said. You can only trust what has been spoken if you trust the nature and character of the One speaking. Faith is not just believing that the Bible has accurate information, it is believing that God is a good God worth trusting. Your trust grows through the experience of walking with God over the years. If you truly believe something then it will change your life. You will act differently. You will plan differently. You will relate differently. And you will pray differently. Hebrews 11:6 says,

> *And without faith it is impossible to please him, for whoever would draw near to God must believe that he exists and that he rewards those who seek him.*

Faith is a gift given from God as a seed in your heart[1]. As you live, act, and minister in proportion to the faith that you have,

---

1   Romans 12:3-8

PERSISTENCE: STAYING FAITHFUL IN PRAYER

your faith begins to grow. Faith is like a muscle that is worked over and over. It grows as you use it. The deeper your trust in God goes, the easier you will find it to live and pray with confident obedience. Through experience, you will discover God is reliable and trustworthy, and the initial seed of faith given to you by the Lord will grow deep roots in our heart, producing a life of holiness, power, and love. This is the result of a vibrant relationship with God. Growing in faith in not proving a theory, it is getting to know a Person.

Jesus connects prayer and faith in a few key teaching moments. In Mark 9, a man brings his demon-possessed son to Jesus for healing and deliverance. The disciples could not help, so the father had to bring his boy to Jesus directly. Jesus cast out the demon and set the boy free. When Jesus was told that his disciples could not cast the demon out, he rebuked the "faithless generation"[2], and when the father asked Jesus if he could help, he replied that anything is possible for those who believe[3]. It seems that the reason the disciples could not deliver the boy was because of their lack of faith. Yet, afterwards, when the disciples were alone with Jesus, they asked him why they weren't able to have an impact. Jesus said, *"This kind can come out by nothing but prayer and fasting."*[4]

What was the issue? Was it prayerlessness or faithlessness? Or was it both? Was the disciples' lack of faith a result of their deficiency in prayer? I think so. You'll notice that when Jesus delivered the boy, he never stopped to pray. He simply cast the demon out. Jesus did not need to organize a prayer rally or call a fast before ministering in power. I believe that's because Jesus was living a lifestyle of prayer and fasting that allowed him to walk in

---

[2] Mark 9:19
[3] Mark 9:23
[4] Mark 9:29 [NKJV]. It's worth noting that other translations only say "prayer" and do not include fasting.

faith, so that he was prepared to minister to people as the needs arose. The disciples had not yet learned to live this way. Because they lacked a consistent prayer life, they lacked faith and could not provide the help that people needed.

The Persistent Widow

This connection between faith and prayer is confirmed in Luke 18:1-8, where Jesus teaches about the need for faithful prayer. It's called the parable of the persistent widow. Unlike some of Jesus's parables, Luke gives away the interpretation before he even begins. In the first verse it says the story was told "that they ought always to pray and not lose heart."

Jesus goes on to describe a poor widow who needed justice from her adversary. She was petitioning an unrighteous judge who did not fear God. After refusing her request for a while, eventually the judge gave in so that she would stop pestering him. In verses 7-8 Jesus drops the punchline:

> *And will not God give justice to his elect, who cry to him day and night? Will he delay long over them? I tell you, he will give justice to them speedily.*

If we are not careful in reading this story, we may think that Jesus is offering us a comparison. Is God like the judge and the church like the widow? Do we need to persist in prayer until we talk God into it? That would be a misunderstanding of Jesus's point in this passage.

Jesus is not offering a comparison, He is offering a contrast. As we have discovered in previous chapters, when we approach God, we are not coming before a stubborn judge. We are coming to our heavenly Father. We are not trying to twist God's arm to bring justice. He desires to make wrong things right more than we do. And we are not coming to him as widows or orphans, but we come to God in prayer as sons and daughters. Verse seven calls us the "elect," which means we are His chosen ones. Jesus wants to remind us that we are adopted.

If your view of God or our own identity becomes skewed, then you will be less likely to keep coming back to Him with consistency. You will easily lose heart in prayer when you lose sight of the nature of the One to whom you go. Yet if you stay rooted in the knowledge of God and your identity in Christ, you will be far less likely to shrink back from His presence, even when you are faced with delays. When you come to God because of who He is, not just what He will do for you, you will keep praying whether your circumstances change or not, because you know that God is ultimately a good, loving and wise Father.

Faithful In Prayer Until the Return of Christ

I am convinced Jesus taught this parable with the prophetess Anna in mind. Anna was a widow who prayed, worshiped, and fasted day and night in the Temple for decades leading up to the first coming of Jesus[5]. Depending on how you do the math, Anna prayed faithfully as a widow for sixty to eighty-four years before Jesus was born.

What on earth would grip a young girl's heart in such a way to keep her steady in prayer for that long? No doubt it was because He wouldn't let her go. She had a revelation of the Messiah. She knew the faithfulness of Yahweh. She had faith in God's promise and did not lose heart.

That same kind of persistent prayer is what Jesus calls his disciples to in the parable about the widow. And Jesus gives them a clue how to do it with his final question in verse eight.

> *Nevertheless, when the Son of Man comes, will he find faith on earth?*

---

[5] Luke 2:36-38

This verse may seem like a random statement; however, Jesus was talking about persistent prayer and the elect, and then He started talking about His second coming and faith. These ideas are related. Jesus was revealing to the listeners that one indicator of faith will be the persistent prayers of His people before He returns. Prayer is an expression of faith. If we believe God is who He says He is and will do what He says He will do, then we will continue to come to Him faithfully in prayer.

You "lose heart" in prayer when you lose faith. You forget who God is and who you are when you become disconnected from His Word. Jesus wants to make sure His followers understand the heart of the Father and their identity in Him. These truths, found in the Word of God, invigorate you to have consistency and joy in your prayer life. In Matthew 21:22 Jesus says:

> "And whatever you ask in prayer, you will receive, <u>if you have faith</u>."

Faith rises in your heart as you behold God in the Scriptures. A revelation of His nature encourages you to engage with Him in prayer, which in turn releases His justice into the earth. Just as Anna partnered with God's promises in faith through prayer before the first coming of Christ, the church at the end of the age will partner with the Spirit of God through persistent, day and night prayer before the second coming of Christ. Will the Son of Man find faith on the earth? Let's make sure the answer is yes!

Dealing With Unanswered Prayers

All of this talk about faith seems great in theory, but let's get real. Sometimes God promises something, you believe it, you ask for it in prayer, but the fulfillment is delayed. And sometimes you ask God for something in prayer, trusting that He wants to do good things, but your prayer is never answered. The challenge of both unanswered and delayed prayers is something that every believer will face.

I learned very early in my walk with God that when you ask Him for things, sometimes He says "yes," sometimes He says "no" and sometimes He says "wait." This trite answer may help you understand the process, but it does little to soothe our souls in a crisis of faith. If God's response to your prayer is "no" or "wait" — particularly if the prayer request is dear to your heart — then you need more substantive answers. It's one thing if God doesn't answer your quick prayer for a good parking spot at the store. It's quite another thing when a child is in the intensive care unit.

> *"If your deepest, most desperate prayers aren't being answered, if life sometimes hurts so much that you secretly wonder whether God exists, and if He does whether He cares, and if He cares why on earth He doesn't just do something to help, then you're not alone." - Pete Greig*[6]

There are many reasons why God may seem to answer "no" or "wait" to our prayers. Greig gives a checklist of fifteen potential reasons for unanswered prayer. He does so cautiously, recognizing the complexity of this topic. He warns that "God Himself interacts with these factors in mysterious ways that invariably confound our nice neat charts and tables!"[7] At the end of the day, there is a sense in which we all have to acknowledge that God's ways are higher than our ways.

With that caveat, his list is still profoundly helpful. He divides unanswered prayer into three categories: God's world, God's will, and God's war.[8] Reasons in God's world for unanswered prayer include the fact that our prayers may be foolish or illogical, or our

---

6   *God on Mute*, Pete Greig
7   *God on Mute*, Pete Greig, pg 261
8   *God on Mute*, Pete Greig, pg 261

prayers could conflict with someone else's prayers, or we may be asking God to spare us from everyday suffering that everyone experiences in a broken world. Reasons in God's will include the fact that our prayers may be selfishly motivated, or God may have something better for us, or we are trying to usurp someone else's will with our prayers. Below we will explore the reasons in God's war — times God might say "wait" rather than a concrete "no." However, if you have lingering questions about unanswered prayers, I highly suggest Greig's book *God on Mute*.

When The Answer is "Wait"

Sometimes God says no, but sometimes you don't know what He is saying. In those moments, there is delay or uncertainty about the answer to your prayers. You find yourself in the space between promise and fulfillment where faith is tested. That is why your faith must first and foremost be rooted in the nature of God. He is good, and He knows best. His timing is perfect, even when you feel like He is late. The delay could be because God wants to cultivate faith in you as you wait. He may use the delay to draw you closer to Himself. Or you may be in the midst of a spiritual battle.

When you are in the realm of unanswered prayers that Greig calls "God's war," remember that there are multiple dynamics at play. First, we need to remember that there is a real, ongoing battle in the spiritual realm between heavenly spirits and demonic spirits. This battle can affect the timing and impact of your prayers.

In Daniel 10, we read an insightful story about an answer to Daniel's prayers being delayed twenty-one days. An angel arrived to tell him that there had been a battle between demonic principalities and angelic forces while Daniel had been praying and fasting. Finally, after three weeks, there was a breakthrough. Daniel 10:12-13 says,

> *Then he said to me, "Fear not, Daniel, for from the first day that you set your heart to understand and humbled yourself before your God, your words have been heard, and I have come because of your words. The prince of the kingdom of Persia withstood me twenty-one days, but Michael, one of the chief princes, came to help me."*

Did you catch that? The angel was dispatched "from the first day" that Daniel began to fast and pray, yet there was a war in the spirit between God's angels and the demonic "prince of Persia". Sometimes your prayers are not answered because you are in the middle of a fight! Prayer and fasting are acts of spiritual warfare. The apostle Paul talks about how we "wrestle" with principalities and powers by putting on the armor of God and "praying at all times in the Spirit"[9]. John Piper says that "one of the reasons prayer malfunctions is because people take a wartime walkie-talkie and try to turn it into a domestic intercom."[10]

We cannot grasp the extent of what is happening in the spiritual realm when we commit to fast and pray. Angels and demons begin to move and shift. There is power and authority released. No wonder we see an increase of miraculous activity. Our prayers are weapons in the spiritual battle between the kingdom of light and the kingdom of darkness.

When in a spiritual war, we will usually feel most discouraged and ready to quit right before the breakthrough comes. Do not stop praying! What would have happened if Daniel had stopped praying on day twenty? I wonder how profoundly that would have altered his life and God's unfolding plan for Israel. I hate to think of how many people have stopped praying early and missed out

---

9 Ephesians 6:12-18
10 https://www.desiringgod.org/interviews/sustain-your-prayer-life-with-sleep - Accessed 04-28-23

on a miracle. I've heard many leaders say, "If you don't quit, you win." That is certainly true with prayer. Mark Batterson says,

> "Our generation desperately needs to rediscover the difference between praying for and praying through. There are certainly circumstances where praying for something will get the job done… But there are also situations where you need to grab hold of the horns of the altar and refuse to let go until God answers."[11]

Older intercessors used to refer to this idea of "praying through." They did not just ask God for something once and then move on, but continued praying until they saw the answer. This was sometimes called "tarrying" in prayer — like the disciples who tarried in the Upper Room until the outpouring of the Holy Spirit. If God has given us a promise in His Word or a prophetic promise over our lives, there will be a battle to see it manifested. God's people must rise up with faith, hold on to God's Word and "pray through."

Prayer Accumulates

Another motivation for persistent prayer is that our prayers never disappear. God never forgets them. I was reminded of this truth when my mom showed me a prayer journal that my grandmother — my Memaw — had written. In it she had written a prayer for me. I was shocked to see God answering her prayers, even years after she had passed away. It was a powerful reminder that our prayers outlive us.

No prayer is wasted. God hears our cries. The Scriptures say that He collects our tears in a bottle[12]. Cornelius was told by an angel that his prayers ascended to God as a memorial.[13] Every

---

11 https://www.markbatterson.com/praying-through/ Accessed 04-28-23
12 Psalm 56:8
13 Acts 10:4

prayer counts before Him. In Revelation 5:8, the apostle John sees the prayers of the saints as incense collected in bowls around the throne of God. They rise to God as a sweet-smelling fragrance. And, in John's vision, these bowls are eventually poured out upon the earth.

This brings us to the shocking realization that prayer accumulates. There are times we pray and pray, and nothing seems to happen. But *something is happening*. Perhaps our prayers for revival, healing, and justice are accumulating in the heavenly bowls. Perhaps they will be poured out in our lifetime, or maybe they will be poured out after we die. Maybe the answers will not fully manifest until Jesus comes again. But we can rest assured God hears our prayers in heaven, and they will impact the earth.

Don't stop praying. Move forward in faith one day at a time. You can trust Jesus. He has come and He will come again. He hears every prayer and will fulfill every promise. In the midst of the battle, pray through. In seasons of delay or unanswered prayer, trust in His good nature and stand on His word. He won't let you go!

Transformation Through Enjoyable Prayer

In the last four chapters, I have shared keys that can help unlock the door to enjoyable prayer in your life. If you will start with worship, pray from the Bible, listen to God's voice, and stay persistent, I promise you that your prayer life will be transformed. As these habits become a part of your relationship with the Lord, He will lead you into what I call the deeper waters of prayer.

In the subsequent chapters, we will explore the depths of intercession, travail, praying in tongues, and fasting. If music, Scripture, listening, and persistence are logs on the fire of your prayer life, then these next chapters will be lighter fluid! If you're hungry for the fullness of all that God has for you, open your heart to the Holy Spirit as you dive into the next section of this book. These dimensions of prayer will not only impact your own heart, but they will ripple into the world around you. This is where prayer becomes transformational.

Part Three: Transformation Through Enjoyable Prayer

NINE

INTERCESSION: PARTNERSHIP WITH GOD IN PRAYER

Four people sat across from me, facing me with smiles. I was at a church in Charlotte, North Carolina, about to receive prophetic ministry for the first time. One of the prophetic words I received there was that God had called me to be a Nazirite. However, the prophetic team did not explain to me what the word "Nazirite" meant—and I had never heard that word before—so I assumed that they had meant "Nazarene." I had never heard the word Nazirite before. When I returned home, I did a quick internet search about nazarenes, to try to understand the significance of the prophetic word. But since I am not from Nazareth or part of the Nazarene denomination, it made no sense to me. I figured they had made a mistake.

Shortly after that time, I was browsing our local Christian bookstore, and I saw a book called *Elijah's Revolution* by Lou Engle and James Goll. I thumbed through it and a chapter title caught my attention: "For the Nazirites to Arise." There was that word. *Nazirite*. Not *Nazarene*. This explained why the prophetic word did not make sense to me.

I immediately purchased the book and read through it quickly — first reading the chapter about Nazirites. I discovered that Nazirites are those throughout history who were uniquely consecrated to God for their lives (such as Samson or Samuel) or for a season of time.[1] Nazirites lived a "fasted lifestyle" that abstained from certain pleasures such as wine in order to be set apart for the Lord.

As I worked through the book, I felt the tangible presence of God multiple times. God was inviting me to pay attention. I had the sense in my heart that the things he was writing about were deeply connected to my own personal destiny. I wanted to learn more about Lou Engle and James Goll. They seemed to be some of the only folks talking about Nazirites, and I knew this was something God had called me to be.

I found a website for Lou Engle's ministry, The Call. They had hosted a gathering on the National Mall in Washington DC in September 2000, where 400,000 people, mostly students, had gathered for a day of fasting, worship, repentance, and prayer for America.[2] I began watching some grainy videos on their website. I heard Lou and other intercessors praying with a fire, desperation, zeal, anointing, and passion that I had never experienced before. It was startling and captivating. Who were these people? How did they learn to pray like this? As I watched, I began feeling God's presence as goosebumps rose all over my skin and tears welled up in my eyes.

One of the videos I clicked on was of Lou's ten-year old son Jesse. He began praying for the Nazirites to arise across America. Immediately my tears began to flow. I started shaking and weeping uncontrollably. For minutes I sat in my computer chair in my room sobbing and trying to keep myself contained. At that moment, through a video on a website, I was receiving an impartation from the Holy Spirit. God was inviting me into a deep

---

1   See Numbers 6
2   The Call hosted similar gatherings in the subsequent years— what they called "solemn assemblies" of prayer and fasting.

place of intercession and marking me as a "Nazirite" to Him. I later understood my experience to be what some call "travailing" in prayer.

This encounter with God was, in many ways, the beginning of my journey as an intercessor. The Holy Spirit deposited something in my heart, and I would never be the same. I had touched a new dimension of prayer that was scary, exciting, beautiful, and overwhelming all at the same time. Despite the intensity of this initial encounter, my subsequent journey into intercessory prayer has brought great joy to my relationship with the Lord. There is something deeply intimate and enjoyable about experiencing the longings of God's heart and partnering with Him to see them manifested in the earth.

Every Christian Is An Intercessor

What exactly is intercession? And what does it mean to be an intercessor? Intercession, or intercessory prayer, is one kind of prayer that Jesus taught us to use in the Lord's Prayer. It is encapsulated in Matthew 6:10 where Jesus says *"your kingdom come, your will be done, on earth as it is in heaven."* The apostle Paul also encourages intercession as one of the key types of Christian prayer available to us in I Timothy 2:1:

> *First of all, then, I urge that supplications, prayers, <u>intercessions</u>, and thanksgivings be made for all people.*

Intercession is simply praying for others. The word "intercede" means to stand in the gap. When we participate in intercessory prayer, we are "standing in the gap" between the Father and the people for whom we are praying. This dimension of prayer is often neglected or misunderstood. Some parts of the body of Christ have relegated intercessory prayer to a small group (usually older women) that meets in the church basement on Tuesday nights. Other churches have abandoned all prayer meetings and prayer ministries completely. Some streams within the church even discourage intercession and mock leaders who are mobilizing intercessory prayer and fasting. The enemy hates intercessors and works hard to discourage and isolate them. The last thing Satan wants is for the church to come into its identity as a Bride who partners with the Holy Spirit in prayer to release God's kingdom on earth.

Yet intercession is part of God's calling for all believers. There is no spiritual gift of intercession. It's not on the lists of gifts and ministries in the New Testament. I believe this is because every Christian should be giving themselves to ministry to the Lord through worship, prayer, and intercession.[3] You are an intercessor. However, just as every Christian is a child of God but does not always live as though they are, many believers are not living as the intercessors that the Lord has designed them to be.

Jesus Is Our Intercessor

The apostle Paul, after instructing Timothy to pray intercessory prayers, reminded him that Christ is the Church's intercessor or mediator. I Timothy 2:5-6 says:

> *For there is one God, and there is one mediator between God and men, the man Christ Jesus, who gave himself as a ransom for all, which is the testimony given at the proper time.*

Jesus is the One who "stands in the gap" between you and the Father. Your prayers and intercession are tied to the ongoing mediation of Christ. Jesus stands forever as the go-between

---

[3] I do believe God has called some to spend *more* time in prayer and intercession, particularly those who are doing ministry vocationally. However, all Christians should be praying all kinds of prayers every day, including intercessory prayers.

INTERCESSION: PARTNERSHIP WITH GOD IN PRAYER

for God and man, and you are invited to stand with Him as an intercessor. You pray to the Father "in Jesus's name" because you cannot come to God otherwise. The answers to your prayers are dependent on the ongoing intercession of the God-man who sits at the right hand of the Father in heaven. This same reality is described in Hebrews 7:25:

> Consequently, he is able to save to the uttermost those who draw near to God through him, since he always lives to make intercession for them.

Jesus is the one who stood in the gap for sinful humanity on the cross, and He continues to intercede for us now. The gap that He fills is the separation between a holy God and sinful humanity. The only solution was for God Himself to come as a man, to bridge the gap and reconcile us to God through His death on the cross, resurrection from the grave, and ascension to heaven. Because of the intercession of Jesus, all who put their faith in Him can be restored back to a right relationship with the Father.

You have a Savior standing in your place, making a way for you to come to God. As Jesus stands in Heaven as our high priest and mediator, I wonder if He is also not whispering prayers of intercession to the Father for the people of the earth? I believe there are conversations, "prayers" if you will, within the Godhead.

Psalm 2 gives us a glimpse of the conversation happening between the Father and the Son regarding the nations of the earth. The psalmist wrote a prophetic song about what would happen — the nations rage against God, the Father exalts His Son as the King, and the nations either worship the Son or come under God's judgment. In the middle of the unfolding drama, the Father speaks to the Son:

> Ask of me, and I will make the nations your heritage.
> Psalm 2:8

The Father tells the Son to ask for the nations, but not because there's a conflict of desires. God wants what God wants. But inside the trinitarian God, the way things get accomplished is through conversations that involve requests. God has chosen to rule the universe through intercession, even within His own being. The eternal heavenly Intercessor, Jesus Christ, is asking the Father for the nations. Jesus is making intercession for you. He is talking to the Father about the fate of your soul. This is stunning!

This perspective is vital for you to enter your intercessory calling as a praying Christian. When you intercede, you are not just asking God for your desires to be released. You are not trying to talk the Father into doing something. You are joining with the intercession of Christ, in unity and partnership with God, to release His kingdom on the earth. This happens through conversation with God about what God wants to do. Mike Bickle says that intercession is when you "use God's words to tell Him what He tells us to tell Him."[4]

Intimacy and Intercession

God has sovereignly chosen to execute His purposes on the earth through the means of intercession. He does not have to wait for you, but He chooses to involve you in His plans. The invitation to intercession is an invitation to partnership and intimacy with God. So while intercession is "praying for others," it is much more than that. It is an intimate partnership with the Lord. It is joining Christ in being a vessel through which God can have his way in the earth.

The prophet Isaiah describes an end-times intercessory prayer movement that will flood the earth before Jesus returns.

> *For as a young man marries a young woman, so shall your sons marry you, and as the bridegroom rejoices over the bride, so shall your God rejoice over you. On your walls, O*

---

4   *Growing in Prayer*, Pg 70

> *Jerusalem, I have set watchmen; all the day and all the night they shall never be silent. You who put the Lord in remembrance, take no rest, and give him no rest until he establishes Jerusalem and makes it a praise in the earth.*
> *Isaiah 62:5-7*

The intercessors here are called watchmen on the wall, and they give God no rest until He establishes His kingdom on the earth. What is the cause of these cries? Intimacy with the Lord. Isaiah describes God relating to His people with covenant love and joy. Before the watchmen are set on the wall of intercession, God rejoices over them as a groom rejoices over a bride. The foundation of their intercessory prayer is a personal, joyful, loving relationship with the Lord.

The pattern is clear: intercession is awakened through intimacy with God. Just as God rejoiced over Israel in Isaiah 62, He rejoices over His people today. The church is the Bride of Christ,[5] and Jesus the bridegroom is delighting in us. As we respond to His invitation and draw near to Him in love, He will awaken an intercessory cry in our hearts. As we stand in the gap with Jesus, our hearts will erupt with the very words He taught us to pray: "Let your kingdom come!"

Three Tensions of Intercession

As a global prayer movement grows, there are certain streams of the body of Christ opposed to asking God for things in intercession. Some leaders actually discourage asking for more of God's kingdom, presence, and power because they wrongly assume that we already have it all. Those who discourage crying out for revival in intercession usually fail to grasp one of the following three biblical tensions that draw us into intercessory prayer.

---

[5] Ephesians 5:32

1. **Personal vs. Corporate Breakthrough.** It is true that we as individual Christians have access to God's Spirit, presence, and power. We are citizens of God's kingdom. We have an "open heaven" over our lives. But just because we, as individual believers, have stepped into these realities does not mean that those around us have. Intercessors are not primarily crying out for their own lives but for those around them who are not experiencing the kingdom of God. The issues of our day beckon intercessors to rise up into their place to ask God for His will to be done on the earth as it is in heaven. Injustice, poverty, unreached people groups, human trafficking, abortion, broken families, and pandemics are ravaging lives. The world is broken, Jesus will heal it, and He wants to move through His praying church to do it.

2. **Kingdom Now vs Not Yet.** The New Testament makes clear that we live in a tension of the kingdom of God that is here but also coming. It is now and not yet. It is breaking in but will also manifest in fullness after Christ returns. So we must embrace the tension of this age. God is with us, but He is not fully with us as He will be in the age to come.[6] If we believe God's kingdom is already here fully, then there is no need for intercession. On the flip side, if we believe that breakthrough is only coming after Jesus returns, then it is useless to pray for God to move right now. However, because the future kingdom is breaking into our present world, intercessory prayer is powerful and transformative.

3. **Jesus's Reign in Heaven vs. Jesus's Reign on the Earth.** The writer of Hebrews expresses this same "now

---

6   Jesus said things like "the hour is coming, and now is" (John 4:23) or "Elijah is coming… but… Elijah has come already." (Matthew 17:11-12)

and not yet" sentiment by describing Jesus's rule and reign like this in Hebrews 2:8: *Now in putting everything in subjection to Him, He left nothing outside his control. At present, we do not yet see everything in subjection to Him.* Jesus rules and reigns in Heaven, but we don't yet see it fully manifested on the earth. This is exactly why Jesus encouraged us to pray for God's kingdom to come on the earth as it is in heaven.

Right in the middle of these three biblical tensions is the place of the intercessor. We stand in the gap between our personal breakthrough in Christ and the breakthrough that God desires for our cities. We stand in the gap between the peace of the kingdom of God that is coming and the turmoil of the present reality around us. And we stand in the gap between Jesus's perfect rule in Heaven and the earth's rebellion against a holy God. In that gap, we ask for God to come and have His way.

Historic revival and moves of God were birthed when God's people became hungry for more of God. They became discontented with what they were currently experiencing in their lives, families, cities, and nations. The message of "I am revival" or "revival is in me" is not the truth that has awakened hearts and sparked nation-shaking Jesus movements. It was a longing for the "fullness of God"[7] that gave birth to historic awakenings and reformations. You can be thankful for what you have experienced in Christ and still hungry for more.

I think Bryan and Katie Torwalt's song "Holy Spirit" does a great job living in this tension of what we have and what we want. It cries out "come flood this place and fill the atmosphere" but also says "let us become more aware of Your presence." It's not just one of these prayers that you should be praying—it's both.

---

7 Ephesians 3:19

We want to be aware of what we already have in Christ, but we also want to desire and cry out for the fullness of what Het has died to give us. So we pray. We ask.

Targeted Intercession

As you launch into intercessory prayer, you may quickly be overloaded by the brokenness and the needs in the world around us. How do you pray? There are so many hurting people and catastrophic current events. There are injustices and crises. There are churches and ministries that need ongoing prayer covering. There are millions of people far from Jesus. You could try to pray for everyone and everything, but that quickly becomes impossible. Perhaps it is easiest to throw up some vague, blanket prayers for the entire world? No. There's a better way.

No one can pray for everything, but God does want you to pray specifically. I believe that God has precise intercessory prayer assignments for believers that help us focus our prayers consistently to bring us deep joy. Jesus is offering an invitation to all Christians to pray for specific people, people groups, needs, and nations. Perhaps one of the reasons you don't enjoy prayer is because you aren't specific and don't know if God is answering you. Jesus promised that answered prayers would be a source of joy. In John 16:24 He says:

> *"Ask, and you will receive, that your joy may be full."*

The Holy Spirit wants to lead you into targeted intercession for specific areas that lead to tangible results which give you joy and faith to continue praying. I use the term "intercessory assignments" to describe the specific people, groups and causes that God leads you to pray for in a targeted and ongoing way. This is not a biblical phrase, but it is a biblical concept. Scripture gives examples of this kind of focused prayer ministry in the prayer lives of Jesus and the apostle Paul.

Jesus' Intercessory Assignment for the Church

The greatest glimpse the Bible gives us into the prayer life of Jesus is His prayer in John 17. This incredible chapter shows us God (the Son) talking to God (the Father).

What did Jesus pray for? Did he pray for everything? Nope. First, Jesus prayed for Himself in verses 1-5, and then Jesus prayed for His disciples in verses 6-19. This is not shocking. We would expect Him to pray first for those who were closest to him. Jesus knew His own needs and the needs of His disciples. He was with them day in and day out.

However, in verse 20 the prayer of Jesus shifts into intercession for the universal church. Jesus prays for us — for all "those who will believe in Me through their word." The Son of God begins to cry out to the Father for the generations yet to come. He begins to labor in prayer for people that He (in His humanity) had not yet met. Jesus was carrying an intercessory assignment for the future church. He didn't even pray for the lost. He prayed for Christians.

While Jesus was on earth, He and the disciples rarely preached to the Gentiles. Instead, they focused their mission on the "lost sheep of the house of Israel" (Matthew 10:5-6). Jesus's earthly preaching ministry was very specific. He had twelve disciples and He preached to the crowds in Israel. Yet part of His prayer ministry was for those in the nations who would come to put their faith in Him. Jesus had received a prayer assignment for people He was not able to preach to at that time.

I believe God is inviting you to follow in the steps of Christ, our great Intercessor, and begin to pray for people you do not know and cannot speak to. He wants to give you intercessory assignments for people you have yet to meet.

Paul's Intercessory Assignment for Israel

Paul is another example of a leader who embraced a specific intercessory prayer assignment. In his letter to the Church of Rome, he reveals a few stunning details about his personal prayer life. Romans 10:1 says:

> Brethren, my heart's desire and prayer to God for Israel is that they may be saved.

Paul is describing his love for the Jewish people and his desire for their salvation. He is praying for them to come to Christ. That is not very surprising, since Paul himself was a Jew. What's interesting to me, though, is that Paul's apostolic ministry of preaching and church-planting was not to the Jews; it was to the Gentiles. Galatians 2:7 makes clear that Paul's apostolic assignment was to "uncircumcised" nations of the earth. It was the apostle Peter who was called to share the Gospel with the Jewish people. So, Paul's ongoing ministry assignment and activity was with the Gentiles nations. He spent his days preaching to Gentiles, making disciples of Gentiles, and planting churches for Gentiles.

Even though Paul's apostolic calling was to the Gentiles, he carried an intercessory assignment for the Jewish people. Most ministers and missionaries spend their prayers focused on the needs of their own churches or the people they are actively trying to reach with the gospel. Paul definitely prayed for those to whom he was ministering. Yet Paul also seemed to be "carrying" the Jewish people in his heart and his prayers, even though He was not called to preach to them. He was still called to pray for them.

Clearly, Paul was burdened and moved emotionally for the Jewish people. He says in Romans 9:2-3:

"...I have great sorrow and continual grief in my heart. For I could wish that I myself were accursed from Christ for my brethren, my countrymen according to the flesh,"

Paul was willing to give up his own salvation to see the Jewish people come to know Jesus! He had truly stepped into that deep place of intercession where he would lay down his own life for those he was praying for. This was, of course, the same thing Jesus did for us when He stood in the gap for us on the cross.

Discerning Your Assignment: Watch Your Tears

The way Paul was moved so deeply for the Jewish people gives us a clue to how we can discern our own intercessory prayer assignments.

Lou Engle says, "Pay close attention to your tears, for your tears point you to your destiny."[8] I believe the Holy Spirit will give you "burdens" for certain things in prayer. If you find yourself tearing up or weeping when you pray for certain people or issues, it is probably because God has given you an intercessory assignment in that area.

I find myself consistently weeping in prayer over two things not directly related to my ministry work: the ending of abortion and the salvation of the Jewish people. I have never been to Israel or ministered to any Jewish people, but I have cried many times praying for them to come to know Jesus (Yeshua) as their Messiah. I have not been touched personally by abortion, but I weep for it to end, especially in America. Nearly every day I pray the Bound4Life prayer: "Jesus, I plead your blood over my sins and the sins of my nation. God, end abortion and send revival to America."[9]

---

8 https://thejesusfast.global/day-7-daniel-sealed-into-my-belly/
9 https://www.bound4life.com/the-life-band/

What stirs your heart? What makes you cry? Perhaps it's a lost family member or friend. Perhaps it's a certain nation or people group. Maybe it's an issue like abortion or human trafficking. It may be a people group or an issue that's unexpected, or it may be something that you're actively involved with. I'd suspect that most of you will receive at least one intercessory assignment that is not directly connected to your own life. God simply wants to share his heart with you and partner with you in the place of prayer. What a deep place of intimacy and partnership that He offers to us!

As you accept your intercessory assignments, be faithful to see them to fruition. If God is giving you a burden to pray, it's because He wants to answer your cries! Labor in prayer in specific ways to see the world around you transformed. I believe this place of intercessory partnership with the heart of God will not only bring you deep joy, but will shift the course of history.

TEN

TONGUES & TRAVAIL: SPIRIT-FILLED PRAYER

It is the Holy Spirit that awakens and empowers love and intercession in God's people, and the activity and power of the Spirit is only going to increase as we near the return of Jesus. The end-times prayer movement will flourish as we welcome the Holy Spirit to move in and among us. Near the end of the Bible, we see a beautiful picture of the partnership that God desires where the Holy Spirit and the Bride of Christ pray together in perfect unity.

> *The Spirit and the Bride say, "Come." Revelation 22:17*

The Church at the end of the age will be in lockstep with God's will and desire. There will be a growing cry from the Spirit-filled Bride to her Groom — "Come!" This global incense of intercession is arising even now. As the world rages with crisis and brokenness, the Church is experiencing the delight of Jesus' love and taking their place on the wall of intercession.

To enter into this flow of intercessory partnership, we must embrace the gift of the Holy Spirit in our midst. He is the One sent from Jesus to empower the church in our mission.[1] He is the One who unites us to Christ and to one another.[2] He is the One

---

1   John 14:16, 26; 15:26, 16:7
2   Ephesians 4:3

who reveals God's love to us,[3] and it is the Spirit who enables effective intercession.

> Likewise the Spirit helps us in our weakness. For we do not know what to pray for as we ought, but the Spirit himself intercedes for us with groanings too deep for words.
> Romans 8:26

If you want to experience the fullness of God's desires for you, invite the Holy Spirit's leadership and activity into your life. You can not enjoy prayer without Him! After all, one of the fruits of the Holy Spirit is joy.[4] The early Church was described as being "filled with joy and the Holy Spirit,"[5] and the kingdom of God is defined as "righteousness and peace and joy in the Holy Spirit." The Holy Spirit is God's presence with us today,[6] and in His presence there is fullness of joy.[7] Enjoyable prayer is Spirit-filled prayer.

Every believer receives the indwelling Holy Spirit in their heart when they put their faith in Jesus,[8] but a relationship with the Holy Spirit is not a one time event. Seek to be baptized in and filled with the Holy Spirit in an ongoing way.[9] In fact, I encourage you to pause reading this book for a few minutes right now, open up your hands to God and ask the Holy Spirit to fill you afresh today. As the Spirit of God fills you, He will empower you to walk in righteousness,[10] to operate in supernatural spiritual gifts,[11]

---

3 Romans 5:5
4 Galatians 5:22
5 Acts 13:52
6 John 14:16-18
7 Psalm 16:11
8 Ephesians 1:13-14
9 Acts 19:2, Ephesians 5:18
10 Galatians 5:16-23
11 See I Corinthians 12

to speak God's word boldly,[12] and to pray as you should.[13] As you develop friendship and familiarity with the presence and power of the Spirit, He will lead you into deeper places of enjoyable prayer.

As you continue to commune with the Holy Spirit daily in the secret place through worship, prayer and the Scriptures, He will fill you with the dreams of God. Just as the Spirit of God "overshadowed" Mary to conceive the Messiah in her womb,[14] the Spirit of God will "overshadow" you with His Word and plant His truth in your heart. It is the physical act of intimacy between a husband and wife that plants a seed in her womb and ultimately leads to the wife giving birth to a child. Likewise, it is spiritual intimacy with God that plants His dreams into your heart by the Holy Spirit. And intercessory prayer is how you see those dreams released into the earth.

Travail: Birthing God's Dreams in Prayer

As God's dreams develop in the womb of your heart, there comes a time when you must spiritually give birth to those growing desires. The birthing process may manifest itself as a kind of travailing intercessory prayer that can be both intensely painful and incredibly joyful. The apostle Paul describes the Spirit of God "groaning" inside believers like a woman who groans in labor pains. Romans 8:20-23 says:

> *For the creation was subjected to futility, not willingly, but because of him who subjected it, in hope that the creation itself will be set free from its bondage to corruption and obtain the freedom of the glory of the children of God. For we know that the whole creation has been groaning together in the pains of childbirth until now. And not only*

---

12 Acts 4:31
13 Romans 8:26
14 Luke 1:35

> *the creation, but we ourselves, who have the firstfruits of the Spirit, groan inwardly as we wait eagerly for adoption as sons, the redemption of our bodies.*

First of all, Paul describes creation groaning for healing from the sin that has corrupted it. This ache for justice and peace is in the hearts of all people, and even in nature itself, to be restored back to God's original purpose without the harmful effects of sin. Then he describes us, as Spirit-filled believers, joining in that groan for Jesus to make all things new. This groaning intercession is the fruit of intimacy with the Lord through the Holy Spirit. God will impart His heart to His people as we co-labor with Him to "birth" His desires into the earth through prayer. Our intercessory prayer is our spiritual "labor" as we cry out day and night.

These groanings are what Corey Russell calls "prayer on the other side of words."[15] He says these deeper prayers available to us through the Holy Spirit include tears, tongues and travail.[16] I believe the groanings that Paul describes above are prayers of travail. To travail means to "engage in painful or laborious effort." Why would there be times that intercession feels painful? The intensity of God's love, desire and passion can be overwhelming for the human spirit to experience. As we encounter deep intimacy with God and begin to feel those longings in his heart, we can be overcome with emotion and even react physically. There are times when the burden of prayer becomes too great to bear.

Have you invited the Holy Spirit to let you feel how He feels? It can be overwhelming. God has the most intense and powerful emotions in the universe. Have you felt God's heart breaking for wrong things to be made right? Have you experienced God's rage against injustice, pain, strife, war, unrighteousness, brokenness,

---

15 https://www.goodreads.com/en/book/show/57641142
16 https://www.youtube.com/watch?v=J8p4UJ-4hUA

and sin? This can wreck the normal flow of your life. It can disrupt business as usual and catch you up into the divine storyline that God is writing for this age — interrupting your emotions and calendars and budgets and priorities.

If you are willing to enter into this, pray the famous prayer: "God, break my heart for what breaks yours." God desires this type of intimacy with you. He wants to touch you more deeply than you realize and share His heart and His secrets with you. He wants a depth of intimate connection that is hard to fathom. He wants you with Him where He is—one with Him, just as the Father and Son are one.[17] This is the place of intimacy and intercession available to you.

Sometimes in these moments of travail, the only thing that can be expressed is a literal groaning or moaning sound. During these moments of travailing prayer, we may bend over or lie on the floor in a fetal position. Often tears will flow. You feel like you have run out of words. You may pray in tongues. Sometimes you may know what you're groaning for, but other times you may not. Yet for those who experience deep intercession like this, it is powerful and intimate.

I believe Paul himself prayed in this way. He wrote to church in Galatia:

> *I am again in the anguish of childbirth until Christ is formed in you! Galatians 4:19*

Elijah also discovered the power of birthing things in prayer. After his showdown at Mt. Carmel, he began to pray for rain. I Kings 18:42 says he *"bowed himself down on the earth and put his face between his knees."* He stayed in that position of travailing prayer until he saw the rain clouds beginning to form in the sky. Putting

---

[17] John 17:20-24

one's head between the knees is actually a natural posture for a woman who is giving birth. Elijah not only took on the heart of birthing prayer, but he literally embodied it.

The apostle James references this story and encourages us to emulate Elijah's prayers of faith. James 5:16-18 says:

> *The prayer of a righteous person has great power as it is working. Elijah was a man with a nature like ours, and he prayed fervently that it might not rain, and for three years and six months it did not rain on the earth. Then he prayed again, and heaven gave rain, and the earth bore its fruit.*

If you begin to experience travail or the sense of birthing something in prayer, I encourage you to continue to pray until you feel a release in your heart that something has truly been birthed. Don't get up until you see the cloud. Surrender to what the Holy Spirit is doing in your heart. You might find yourself wanting to lie on the floor or get on your knees. Many people rock forward and backward as they pray. As in real childbirth, the physical and emotional sensations can be all-consuming. I personally have felt a literal tightness in my belly during travailing prayer, even such that my stomach was sore for a few days afterwards.[18]

Entering these deep places of travailing intercession is a gift from God. Though it can be painful at times, it is also a joyful privilege. Jesus said in John 16:21,

> *When a woman is giving birth, she has sorrow because her hour has come, but when she has delivered the baby, she no longer remembers the anguish, for joy that a human being has been born into the world.*

---

18 For all the moms out there, I am by no means saying that intercession is equivalent in intensity or pain to actual childbirth!

Likewise, the intensity of travailing prayer gives way to incredible joy when we see God's dreams birthed into the world. To experience such nearness to God and to participate with Him in knowing His heart is one way we can enjoy prayer more fully. Intercession in our own strength is exhausting, but Spirit-filled intercessory prayer that flows from intimacy with God is exciting and satisfying to our souls — because we get to know Him more and partner with Him to transform the world through prayer.

Praying in the Spirit

The same Holy Spirit that groans within us empowers us with spiritual gifts[19]. The spiritual gift of tongues is uniquely connected to prayer. Like travailing prayer, tongues is another kind of prayer "on the other side of words." Paul teaches about praying in tongues in I Corinthians 14:13-15. He says:

> *Therefore let him who speaks in a tongue pray that he may interpret. For if I pray in a tongue, my spirit prays, but my understanding is unfruitful. What is the conclusion then? I will pray with the spirit, and I will also pray with the understanding. I will sing with the spirit, and I will also sing with the understanding.*

There are times when the gift of tongues manifests as a supernatural ability to speak a language you don't know, such as on the day of Pentecost.[20] There are other times that the gift of tongues manifests as unknown heavenly languages. In the passage above, praying "with the spirit" is utilizing a heavenly prayer language – what Paul also calls the tongues of angels.[21] In these instances, the Holy Spirit is supernaturally empowering you to

---

19   See I Corinthians 12 and Romans 12
20   Acts 2:4-6
21   I Corinthians 13:2

pray with sounds and syllables that do not make any sense to your natural mind.

In church gatherings these heavenly languages can sometimes be interpreted. The rest of the passage in I Corinthians 14 goes into detail about the proper protocol for the interpretation of tongues in public meetings. There are also times that the gift of tongues is not meant for others. In these instances, the gift of tongues is for your personal edification. I Corinthians 14:4 says "The one who speaks in a tongue builds up himself." How exactly are you edified by unknown words? Why would you want to pray using languages that you do not understand?

The phrase "builds up" in verse 4 is sometimes translated "edify." Edify comes from the word edifice – meaning a building or structure. As you pray and sing in tongues you are building yourself up and literally creating space in your spirit to receive revelation from God. Many times as you pray in tongues you begin to receive revelation and understanding from the Lord. He may release visions, ideas, wisdom and insights as you pray. This is why Paul encourages us to seek an understanding of what is being said: *"...let him who speaks in a tongue pray that he may interpret."*

The impact of prayer in tongues is mainly in the spirit realm. You may or may not know exactly what is happening as you pray this way, but you can be sure the Spirit is moving through you to release His will.[22] Jude confirms that Spirit-filled prayer is a way for a believer to build themselves up. Jude 20 says:

> *But you, beloved, building yourselves up on your most holy faith, praying in the Holy Spirit.*

The "place" that is built as we pray in tongues is our hearts — our spirit man. When Paul encouraged us to pray "with the spirit,"

---

[22] Romans 8:26-27

he was referring to praying with our hearts connected to the Spirit of God. In the original Greek language, the same word is used for the spirit of man and the Spirit of God. God's Spirit is "pneuma." Your spirit is also "pneuma." Paul says to pray with the pneuma. Jude says to pray with the pneuma.

As the Spirit of God flows through your heart, strength and faith will rise. Revelation and understanding will come. Through the power of the Holy Spirit you can pray both in your native language and in supernatural tongues to build yourself up in faith.

Tongues as Spiritual Warfare

Praying in the spirit is also an act of spiritual warfare. At the end of Paul's passage on the armor of God, praying in the Spirit is mentioned along with the word of God as a key to spiritual victory:

> ...*praying always with all prayer and supplication in the Spirit, being watchful to this end with all perseverance and supplication for all the saints. Ephesians 6:18*

It may seem superstitious to talk of Satan, angels and demons in the twenty-first century, but our ancestors were well aware of the spiritual beings that energize the world around us. We ignore the invisible spiritual battle happening all around us to our own detriment. Satan is real, and his goal is to steal, kill and destroy.[23] You can either recognize the battle that is raging and get in the fight, or you can pretend that it doesn't exist and wonder why your life keeps getting derailed. You don't want to give the devil too much credit, but you also don't want ignorance of spiritual warfare to hinder God's best for you.

If you're willing to engage in the battle, then start praying in the spirit. As Paul said earlier, *"pray with the spirit, and.... with the*

---
23 John 10;10

understanding…sing with the spirit, and…with the understanding." The enemy hates when believers pray and sing in tongues. And the beauty of this spiritual gift is that you may not even be aware of the war that is raging around you as you pray. You can simply focus on the Lord, allow the Holy Spirit to flow and watch Him fight on your behalf.

Jesus was no stranger to spiritual warfare. He taught the Lord's Prayer shortly after his encounter with Satan in the desert during his forty-day fast. With this experience fresh on his mind, He includes a prayer of spiritual warfare in his model prayer for us: "And do not lead us into temptation, but deliver us from the evil one."[24]

Interestingly, Jesus does not teach us to speak to the enemy, but to speak to the Father about the enemy. You can wrestle the enemy most effectively by focusing on and interacting with the Lord rather than focusing on and interacting with demonic forces.[25] Ask God to deliver you from the evil one. There are times you should engage the enemy directly,[26] but that should be minimal compared to the time you spend talking with God directly. Your default prayer of warfare should be "The Lord rebuke you!"[27]

This is why the gift of tongues is such a blessing. When you pray in tongues, you might not even be aware that warfare is even happening. But you can pray in faith that God knows what you need and is fighting for the battle. The Holy Spirit will help you in

---

24 Matthew 6:13
25 When we minister to others, there may be times that should cast out demons from people, just as Jesus and the apostles did. Demons in individuals can be cast out. But we wrestle with the principalities and powers that Paul described above. We should not wrestle when it's a moment to cast out, and we should not try to cast out the things with which we are to wrestle.
26 Matthew 16:23, Acts 16:18, etc.
27 Jude 1:9

your weakness. Invite Him to fill you again and lead you into the intimate, intense and exhilarating prayer beyond words.

FASTING: HUNGER FOR GOD THROUGH PRAYER

It was the day of a citywide, outdoor prayer event called Day Seven. Our small worship ministry had spent the spring traveling to various youth groups and churches to host worship and revival nights for students. The culmination of our trip was a big night of worship and prayer at the amphitheater of our Town Common — the biggest park in our city. In the days leading up to the event, our team kept an eye on the weather forecast. It called for rain. After several months of planning and preparation, we would be devastated to have our gathering canceled due to bad weather. We decided to continue with the event in faith, praying that the rain would hold off and the clouds would clear.

We named the event Day Seven because we called for seven days of fasting and prayer leading up to the gathering. Our theme was the story of Joshua at Jericho. We were praying for the metaphorical "walls" to fall down around our city as we united in prayer, worship, fasting, and obedience. I had never fasted for seven days, but I figured this was a good time to start. I was in my early twenties, and I did not trust myself to have enough self-control to avoid food for seven days. But I knew the accountability of doing it with others would help me stay faithful.

Our team arrived at the park on the seventh day to unload gear and set everything up. Dark clouds were looming. We were all fasting, hungry, and exhausted. But we were also full of faith, expectant and desperate for God to do something in our lives and city. Throughout the afternoon set up and sound check, rain fell off and on. We had tents and tarps to cover everything the best we could. Intercessors walked around on site, doing their best to pray away the rain.

When it was time for worship to begin, the crowd gathered and the rain stopped. In fact, right above the park the clouds parted and the blue sky was visible. Miraculously, God provided a physical and spiritual "open heaven" for our night of prayer. We were ecstatic to see God move in a way that seemed like the kind of thing you only read in Bible stories. The sea parted for Moses. Jesus walked on water. Elijah called fire from heaven. Joshua saw the sun stand still. And we saw clouds part, in the middle of a storm, so that we could gather the students of our city together to worship and pray for revival. Later that night, I found a video of the weather radar, and you could clearly see the storms moving towards Greenville and splitting right over us during that time. Needless to say, this was an eye-opening experience for me regarding the power of prayer and fasting.

The Neglected Discipline of Fasting

I am convinced that fasting is one of the neglected keys for awakening a lukewarm western church and keeping our hearts hungry for God even in the midst of our prosperity. I believe a fasting and praying people will be who God uses to give birth to the revival He longs to release. As we near the return of Christ, the Bride's desire for Christ and His kingdom will grow in intensity.[1]

---

1 Matthew 9:15

The Holy Spirit will fan the flame and release grace to the body of Christ to fast and pray like never before.

Fasting is like a nitro boost for your prayer life. I once heard someone say that fasting and prayer go together like peanut butter and jelly (the irony of comparing fasting to a food is not lost on me). Fasting and prayer are paired together throughout the Bible because they are a powerful combination to awaken your heart and increase the potency of your prayers. Fasting may not seem enjoyable — while you're in the moment. But the rewards are great. In our Christian walk, sometimes the deepest joys come after doing the hardest things.

Fasting Regularly is Normal Christianity

Most Christians do not think about fasting as a normal Christian discipline, but it will become normal again. As we will see, fasting is not just a special event. Yes, there are times to come together for seasons of focused fasting and prayer during a crisis. But God desires a people who fast and pray as a lifestyle.

The Sermon on the Mount (Matthew 5-7) is Jesus's foundational teaching on the kingdom of God. This was essentially his Christianity 101 class. In this broader teaching, Jesus considered fasting a normal part of what it meant to be a follower of God. He included fasting along with other accepted Christian disciplines such as prayer and doing good deeds.[2]

In this passage Jesus confronted the hypocrisy and legalism of the Jewish people in that day and age.

He began by correcting their approach to giving:

> *"when you give to the needy..." Matthew 6:2*

He then offers a correction to hypocritical prayer:

> *"when you pray..." Matthew 6:5*

---

[2] Matthew 6:1-18

Jesus's assumption here is that followers of God are going to be giving and praying. He does not even need to encourage them to do it. He was simply correcting their approach. After teaching on giving and prayer, he gives his third correction:

> *"when you fast..." Matthew 6:16*

Jesus did not make fasting an option for His followers. He assumed we would be doing it — *when* you fast, not *if* you fast. Giving, prayer, and fasting are some of the basic practices of Jesus' foundational teaching about being in the kingdom of God. And Jesus's early followers heeded his instruction.

The Church at Antioch "ministered to the Lord and fasted" in Acts 13:2. As I mentioned before, the original word used in that verse about Antioch for ministry is the Greek word where we get the English word liturgy. In other words, their ministry to the Lord with worship, prayer, and fasting was their regular practice. Historical sources such as the Didache indicate that the early Church continued the practice of devout Jews to fast two days per week.[3]

It is easy to see the contrast between the early Church and modern western evangelicalism. In our day, those who fast and pray even sparingly are considered radical Christians. Many believers have never heard a sermon on fasting. Many have never tried fasting as a way to worship and pursue God. And even fewer practice it as a regular spiritual discipline like the early church. Yet Jesus indicated that it should be just as normal as prayer or giving. No one believes that Christians should only give or pray sporadically. Most Christians rightly believe that we should pray daily and regularly give to those in need. Jesus teaches us that fasting should be a regular Christian activity too.

---

[3] See Luke 18:12

The easiest way to embrace a fasted lifestyle is to fast weekly. I suggest you start with skipping lunch one day each week and using that time for prayer and Bible reading. This simple step is a powerful way to begin your journey into regular fasting. It's important that you spend time with the Lord when you would normally eat. You are not just trying to skip meals. You want to draw closer to God.

As it becomes more normal to skip a meal, you can move towards two meals. My preference is to skip breakfast and lunch. I eat dinner one evening and then fast until dinner on the next night. This allows me to fast for about twenty-four hours each week. You can experiment with what works best for you. Perhaps you will want to build up to fasting for two days each week like the early church and other Christians throughout history.

Fasting Accesses What Jesus Died to Give

> *"Do not be afraid, Abram. I am your shield, your exceedingly great reward." Genesis 15:1*

The greatest reward the Father gives those who fast is Himself. God is the reward. He is the One who ultimately satisfies our souls. When Jesus discouraged hypocritical prayer and fasting in Matthew 6, he drew a line between those who found their reward in people's approval and those who found their reward from the Father's approval.

> *And when you fast, do not look gloomy like the hypocrites, for they disfigure their faces that their fasting may be seen by others. Truly, I say to you, they have received their reward. But when you fast, anoint your head and wash your face, that your fasting may not be seen by others but by your Father who is in secret. And your Father who sees in secret will reward you. Matthew 6:16-18*

Jesus says to fast "in secret" before God Himself. Fasting should be an expression of your hunger for God, your desire to love God, and your willingness to obey Him. Fasting should be Godward. The prophetess Anna "worshiped [or served] God with fasting."[4] Fasting is an expression of your worship and ministry to the Lord, along with praise and prayer.

Fasting "in secret" does not mean that you cannot let anyone know that you are fasting. It does mean you should be discrete and avoid drawing unnecessary attention to yourself. Jesus was primarily dealing with motivations and principles more than setting rigid rules. The motive for why you are fasting is the important issue to Jesus.

Fasting to please men is not true, biblical fasting. If you're fasting to seem super spiritual to others or to try to earn God's love, or to punish yourself for your sins, then you're missing the point. God's grace is a free gift. Jesus died and rose again to set you free from sin and restore you to a right relationship with God. Fasting doesn't earn what Jesus already paid for on the cross. When you put your faith in Christ, you are clothed in His righteousness. It is not your merit through fasting or anything else that justifies you before God. It is what He has already done for you.

In light of the gospel, fasting falls into the category of activities that Bible teachers call "means of grace." There are certain biblical ways that God chooses to release his grace and power to His people. Prayer, Bible reading, baptism, church, serving others, communion, etc. can all be seen as means of grace. It's not that doing these things *earns* God's grace. It's that doing these things *accesses* His grace. A child opening a gift isn't earning the gift by the act of unwrapping. It is just the only proper way to accept the free gift. You have to (get to!) unwrap it to receive

---

4   Luke 2:37

it. Fasting and other spiritual disciplines are how you unwrap the gift of God's grace and power in your life.

Fasting Expresses and Cultivates Hunger for Jesus

In God's providence there is a link between our physical hunger and our spiritual hunger. When you obey Jesus's invitation to fast and pray, you begin to awaken deep hunger in your heart for God. And that hunger makes you want to fast, which makes you hungrier for Him. Fasting both expresses and cultivates spiritual hunger. That perpetual longing — carried in the hearts of those who embrace a fasted lifestyle — is actually a normal heart posture for Christians. The betrothed Bride of Christ is to be lovesick for Jesus.

The reality is that you have limited capacity, and it is only as you empty yourself through fasting and prayer that you can be filled with God and experience true satisfaction. You can only be deeply satisfied if you first awaken deep hunger. C.S. Lewis says,

> "It would seem that our Lord finds our desires not too strong, but too weak. We are half-hearted creatures, fooling about with drink and sex and ambition when infinite joy is offered us, like an ignorant child who wants to go on making mud pies in a slum because he cannot imagine what is meant by the offer of a holiday at the sea. We are far too easily pleased."[5]

In one sense fasting "satisfies" you as you experience more of God's presence, revelation from Scripture, a joy in prayer, and a sense of deep intimacy with the Lord. In another sense, fasting makes you unsatisfied. As the old song says, "the more I find You, the more I want You."[6] This is the cry of a lovesick Bride.

---

5   *The Weight of Glory*, CS Lewis
6   *The More I Seek You* by Zach Neese

ELEVEN

> *"To have found God and still to pursue Him is the soul's paradox of love."* AW Tozer[7]

The tension of the "already" and "not yet" of God's presence creates a yearning inside of believers. As Christians, we have the Holy Spirit with us, yet we long for the physical return of Jesus and the consummation of His kingdom. The Spirit is the down payment — the "guarantee of our inheritance"[8] — but we want the full payment. The Holy Spirit is like an engagement ring, and we are anticipating the ceremony. Like a bride awaiting her wedding day, we cannot wait for Jesus to descend to Earth and culminate what He began in His first coming.

Jesus knew that we would feel that tension and he describes it as "mourning." The fasting Bride aches for more of Jesus. Here's what He says about this:

> Then the disciples of John came to Him, saying, "Why do we and the Pharisees fast often, but Your disciples do not fast?" And Jesus said to them, "Can the friends of the bridegroom mourn as long as the bridegroom is with them? But the days will come when the bridegroom will be taken away from them, and then they will fast. Matthew 9:14-15

In the context of this passage, the Pharisees criticized Jesus because his disciples did not fast. His rebuttal was that they would fast after he was "taken away from them." Jesus's point is this: when He was with His disciples in the flesh, there was no need to fast because they were satisfied with His presence. However, when He ascended to heaven, as He is now, Jesus predicted that His disciples would fast because they would hunger for His return, His presence, and His kingdom.

---

7   *The Pursuit of God* by AW Tozer
8   Ephesians 1:13-14

We are now in the day that Jesus foresaw. This is the time that we should be hungering for more of Him. Jesus makes it clear that the church will fast until He returns to earth again. Fasting is a way that we as the Bride of Christ anticipate, hasten,[9] and prepare for the Lord's return.[10]

Embracing Voluntary Weakness and Dependence

In a previous chapter I discussed the important relationship between prayer and faith. A lifestyle of ongoing prayer, Scripture meditation and fasting will allow you to walk in a measure of faith to see God's miraculous power released in your life and those within your influence. I believe the reason this happens is that fasting heightens awareness of your weakness and neediness before God.

When you become desperate and vulnerable, you have no choice but to lean into God for His supernatural strength. The truth is, you are always needy, but fasting exposes the reality of the ongoing situation in your soul. Fasting regularly allows you to stay in perpetual awareness of your dependence on His grace.

Jesus is the perfect example of this. As you recall, Jesus could cast the demon out of the boy, and he rebuked his disciples for a lack of faith. He said that some only come out by prayer and fasting.[11] Yet Jesus did not stop to call a fast or a prayer meeting. He was living a fasted and prayerful lifestyle. He was ready to act in faith when the need arose, and therefore miracles followed Him everywhere He went. God wants the same thing for you and me.

---

9   2 Peter 3:12
10   Jesus seems to use the bride/bridegroom analogy specifically when it relates to His second coming. See Matthew 25:1-13 as well as references throughout the book of Revelation.
11   See Chapter 8

If you will begin to embrace rhythms of fasting in your life, I believe you will see an uptick of supernatural activity, miracles, dreams, visions, healings, and other gifts of the Spirit. You will become more attuned to the voice of God and more aware of His presence with you. In your weakness, God will be strong.[12]

The Power of United Fasting and Prayer

As churches and communities unite in prayer and fasting, we will see an even greater move of the Spirit in our cities and nations. Throughout Church history, united fasting and prayer preceded great revival, and the greatest move of God is yet to come. Derek Prince says,:

> *"Today, God's Spirit is being poured out in a measure… But as yet, we only see a small fraction of the total outpouring that the Bible clearly predicts. God is waiting for us to meet His requirements. It will take united prayer and fasting to precipitate the final fullness of the latter rain."*[13]

Prince was reflecting on the call to united prayer and fasting in Joel 2. Joel was a prophetic voice to Israel in a season of national crisis. God spoke through the prophet to call His people to humble themselves, repent of their sins, fast and pray. He promised to pour out His Spirit and release His blessings if they would turn to Him with all their hearts. Are we in a crisis in our day and time? AW Tozer has said, *"The fall of man has created a perpetual crisis."*[14] Therefore, our perpetual response, until Christ returns, should be to fast and pray.

The prescription of united prayer and fasting laid out in Joel 2 was adopted in the Upper Room of Acts 2. As Jesus' disciples waited for the Holy Spirit in united prayer (and likely fasting) for ten days, they may have even reflected on the prophetic promises

---

12   2 Corinthians 12:10
13   *Shaping History Through Prayer and Fasting*, page 129
14   *Tozer on Christian Leadership* by A.W. Tozer, copyright © 2001

found there. Because when the day of Pentecost came, the Holy Spirit released fire upon the church, and Peter stood up to quote Joel to explain the phenomena.

> For these people are not drunk, as you suppose, since it is only the third hour of the day. But this is what was uttered through the prophet Joel: "'And in the last days it shall be, God declares, that I will pour out my Spirit on all flesh, and your sons and your daughters shall prophesy, and your young men shall see visions, and your old men shall dream dreams; even on my male servants and female servants in those days I will pour out my Spirit, and they shall prophesy. And I will show wonders in the heavens above and signs on the earth below, blood, and fire, and vapor of smoke; the sun shall be turned to darkness and the moon to blood, before the day of the Lord comes, the great and magnificent day. And it shall come to pass that everyone who calls upon the name of the Lord shall be saved.'"
> Acts 2:15-21

What had been promised began that day. As God's people humbled themselves in prayer, God poured out His Holy Spirit. Tongues of fire manifested on the heads of the people. They spoke in unknown languages so that foreigners could understand the Gospel. The fearful walked in boldness and power. In short: revival had broken out.

But Peter wanted them to understand something: it happened for a reason. The promise of an outpouring of God's Spirit was a conditional promise. Only if God's people responded rightly would they see the miraculous power of God. 120 of Jesus's followers were in the upper room and prepared for what God wanted to do. We can assume that if they were not, then Pentecost, as we know it, would have been delayed.

The same call to humble, repentant prayer and fasting can be found in 2 Chronicles 7:14.

> **If** My people who are called by my name humble themselves, and pray and seek my face and turn from their wicked ways, **then** I will hear from heaven and will forgive their sin and heal their land.

If we humble ourselves. *If* we pray. *If* we seek His face. *If* we turn from our sins. Then He will begin to move. This is something that God wants to do. He wants revival and awakening more than we do. But He can only move through vessels who have been humbled and purified in the furnace of fasting and prayer. When this verse says, "humble themselves," it could just as easily say "fast." In Psalm 69:10 David said, *"I wept and humbled my soul with fasting."* This humility, and the faith that comes with it, is vital for us to steward the amazing outpouring of God's Spirit that He wants to release in our lives and across the earth.

If you want to walk in faith, see miracles, and experience more of God's power and presence in your life, I urge you to embrace fasting and prayer. As you do, you will have faith to be used by God in powerful ways, and your prayers could even shift the future of nations. If you are struggling to see breakthroughs with your personal life, family members, cities, or nations, perhaps fasting and prayer is what we need to move the spiritual powers in the heavenlies and release God's purposes.

Note that fasting is not to be approached casually. It is not suitable for all people at all phases of life. Always consult your doctor and local church leadership for guidance before engaging in any kind of intense fasting. I do not have space in the book to provide a lot of practical tips or guidance on fasting in a healthy way. However, we have created a downloadable "Practical Suggestions for Fasting" document at enjoyingprayer.com. *Please read through it before beginning your journey into fasting.*

Part Four: The House of Enjoyable Prayer

TOGETHER: THE NEED FOR CORPORATE PRAYER

If you ever crave pancakes at three a.m., there is at least one place you can go anytime day or night to get them: The International House of Pancakes. In most cities across America, the restaurants are open twenty-four hours a day. And you can rest assured that they will have pancakes—it says so right in their name. If you pulled up to IHOP to satisfy your craving, you would be rightfully frustrated and confused if they did not have any pancakes available. It would be nonsensical for a pancake house to fail to offer the item that is part of their very identity. Of course, IHOP has more than pancakes—they offer sandwiches, steaks, eggs, and all kinds of food. But their specialty is pancakes. If you want pancakes, they have you covered.

Where am I going with this? Listen to the statement that Jesus made in multiple Gospels:

> *'My house shall be called a house of prayer'*[1]

We are a house of prayer. This is central to our identity as the church. This does not mean that prayer is the only thing that we do. Just as IHOP has a wide variety of food on their menu, churches should have a variety of ministries and activities. However, many

---

1 Matthew 21:13, Mark 11:17, Luke 19:46

churches do not even have prayer on the menu, so to speak. Yet Jesus said that prayer should be our specialty.

As Jesus looks across the landscape of western Christianity, how do you think He would describe His people? If He looked at how we prioritize our time, attention, resources, and energy, what would He call us? A house of what? A house of preaching? A house of community service? A house of evangelism? A house of pastoral care? A house of discipleship? A house of fellowship?

I can't imagine He would call us a house of prayer. Yet He has declared that that is who we are, and that is who we will become. Our conversation with Him, our love for Him, our interaction with Him, the power that flows through us in intercession, our extravagant devotion to Him — these activities will be what Jesus and the world sees when they see the Christian church. Jesus has promised it, and He will have His way. The church will function as the house of prayer that we are.

Joy In The House of Prayer

Jesus quoted this prophecy from Isaiah while violently clearing out the Temple. For most of us, this is one of the most uncomfortable scenes in the life of Jesus. He fashioned a whip, turned over tables, and confronted the individuals who had altered the Temple from a place of worship into a place for personal profit. The Jewish "church" had become transactional and consumeristic, instead of a place for prayer and sacrifice. Jesus was unusually angry and confrontational, yet He did not sin. The jealous love of our Savior was on full display. He was passionate to have people who seek Him and worship Him with pure hearts. In a similar story in John 2 (some people say it is the same story), Jesus confronted those in the Temple again. His disciples, observing the fervor of Jesus, quote Psalm 69:9: "Zeal for your house will consume me."[2] Zeal for what house consumed Jesus? The house of prayer. The church. This is what burns in His heart for us.

To step into our identity as Jesus's house of prayer, we have to stop viewing prayer as only individualistic. Corporate prayer must become a normal part of our rhythms and routines. Whether it be groups of friends, small groups, campus ministries, or prayer rooms, it is time to engage God together.

The idea of praying with others may feel awkward or boring to you. Praying out loud in front of other people might seem intimidating. Maybe you have never attended a prayer meeting that was refreshing, energizing, and powerful. I have been to some awkward and boring prayer meetings, so I understand the hesitancy. For some humorous examples, check out the article titled "Seven Ways to Ruin A Prayer Meeting" at enjoyingprayer.com.

However, God is not boring. In His presence there is fullness of joy![3] Remember that God promised in Isaiah 56:7 to make us joyful in the *house* of prayer. If we can learn to pray together in God's presence, with worship at the center, we will experience deeper joy in our prayer lives. Jesus's incredible promise means that we can come together with other believers, seek God in prayer, and enjoy ourselves. It is possible! Let us press into that joy together.

Corporate Prayer in Acts

The apostles and early followers of Jesus evidently understood Jesus's desire was for them to be praying together regularly. Corporate prayer is a major theme in the book of Acts.

---

2 John 2:17
3 Psalm 16:11

After Jesus' ascension, the apostles first activity was gathering to pray until Pentecost (Acts 1:14).

Prayer continued to be one of the primary activities at church gatherings after Pentecost (Acts 2:42).

The Jewish believers continued to go to the temple to pray together to Yahweh (Acts 3:1, 22:17).

The church gathered to pray in response to persecution and were baptized in fresh power and boldness to minister to others (Acts 4:23-31).

The apostles found themselves distracted by feeding the poor, so they delegated some of their ministry responsibilities and returned to prayer and God's Word as their primary ministry work (Acts 6:4).

The church united in a home to offer "constant prayer" for Peter together (Acts 12:5, 12).

The church gathered to minister to God in Antioch with worship, prayer and fasting (Acts 13:1-3).

There was a well-known "place of prayer" near the river (Acts 16:13,16).

Paul and Silas were stuck in jail so they reverted to what they knew to do — they worshiped and prayed (Acts 16:25-34).

Paul gathered with the church at Ephesus and Tyre to pray (Acts 20:36, 21:5).

A culture of prayer permeates the book of Acts, and nearly every reference is related to the church praying *together*. Jesus taught His disciples to engage in corporate prayer. He identified His people as a house of prayer. The early church prayed together in regular, frequent rhythms. And as Christianity spread, the apostles continued to urge the churches, through their letters, to be faithful in corporate prayer.

Prayer In The New Testament Epistles

As you read the verses below, I want you to understand how they would have been received. These church communities would have been hearing instructions to them as a group. They would understand these calls to prayer as a call to corporate prayer.

Paul asked the Romans to *"strive together with me in prayers."*[4] He was giving them a corporate intercessory prayer assignment.

In his teaching to the Corinthian church about orderly church gatherings, he tells them to *"pray with the spirit, and...pray with the understanding."*[5] Praying in their native language and "with the spirit"[6] were both to be normal parts of the church's activity together.

He urges the Church at Ephesus to be *"praying always with all prayer and supplication in the Spirit, being watchful to this end with all perseverance and supplication for all the saints."*[7]

To the believers in Phillipi he says *"Be anxious for nothing, but in everything by prayer and supplication, with thanksgiving, let your requests be made known to God."*[8]

The Colossians were also taught to pray: *"Continue earnestly in prayer, being vigilant in it with thanksgiving."*[9]

Likewise, the apostle James encouraged the communities of Jewish believers in corporate prayer: *"Is anyone among you suffering? Let him pray... confess your sins to one another and pray for one another, that you may be healed. The prayer of a righteous person has great power as it is working."*[10]

---

5 Romans 15:13
5 I Corinthians 14:15.
6 See chapter 11 for more on praying in the spirit
7 Ephesians 6:18
8 Phillipians 4:6
9 Colossians 4:2
10 James 5:13-16

Peter's letters to the churches in Asia Minor follow the same pattern. He says, *"But the end of all things is at hand; therefore be serious and watchful in your prayers."*[11]

Not surprisingly, the apostle John tells a group of churches *"that if we ask anything according to His will, He hears us. And if we know that He hears us, whatever we ask, we know that we have the petitions that we have asked of Him."*[12]

Nearly every New Testament book commands the church to pray, and nearly every reference is to be understood corporately. Even Jesus Himself taught us to pray together. The Lord's prayer begins with "Our Father" not "My Father." Because we are called to pray together.

Confronting Individualism

To shift your mindset and embrace corporate prayer, you have to let go of the individualistic approach to Christianity that is so common in the west. The idea that following Jesus is something you can do on your own is not a biblical concept. Yes, you must have a personal faith and individual relationship with God. It is true you must choose, on your own, to trust Christ or not. However, when you choose to follow Him, you are choosing to do so as part of the body of Christ. Just as a spouse marries into their spouse's family, you marry into the church — crazy uncles included!

When you read the New Testament, it is vital not to interpret everything as if it is applying to you individually. When Paul was writing letters to the churches, he was writing to the congregations, not to individuals. The instructions and encouragements were to be embraced corporately by the community. The local churches heard God's word to them through Paul and had to work out

---

11   I Peter 4:7 [NKJV]
12   I John 5:14-15

obedience together. This puts an entirely different spin on so many verses that we try to fulfill on our own.

For instance, when Paul encourages the believers at Thessalonica to "pray without ceasing,[13]" he is not primarily telling each individual believer to pray constantly. Some people have taken the command to pray ceaselessly to mean that each of us should try to be aware of God's presence throughout our day, to pray sporadically as we go along, and to abide in Christ in our hearts as much as possible. That is great! Brother Lawrence called this "practicing the presence" of God.[14] However, Paul is also encouraging the church to pray all the time *collectively*. And even a small local church could fulfill this command literally if members of the church took shifts to pray around the clock. We will talk more about this in the next chapter.

Praying Better Together

One benefit I have found from corporate prayer is that I pray more when I pray with others. Some days you feel passion for God and some days you feel weary. This is totally normal. Yet committing to praying with others allows you to be stirred up to do what you know you should be doing.

On the days one person feels tired and weary, inevitably someone else will feel energized. And on other days, the previously energized people will be tired and need some encouragement from someone else. As you gather to pray, the overall "water level" rises because those around you encourage you to do more than you would if you were on your own.

> And let us consider how to stir up one another to love and good works, not neglecting to meet together, as is the habit of some, but encouraging one another, and all the more as you see the Day drawing near. Hebrews 10:24-25

---

13 1 Thessalonians 5:17
14 See *The Practice of the Presence of God* by Brother Lawrence

Churches and communities that pray together also pray more individually. Your private times with God will get better when you have been around other believers in worship and prayer. Being in the presence of God refuels you and impacts your entire life. What happens during prayer meetings is only just the beginning. There are ripple effects into families and communities when God's people come together to pray and worship.

Not only do you tend to pray more when you pray together, but you usually pray for a greater variety of things. When you only pray on your own, you can easily overlook certain things that are very important to the Lord. However, when you work together as the body of Christ, you can more fully grasp all that is on God's heart.

One person may focus on giving thanks to the Lord, and everyone at the meeting can join with them in thanksgiving. Another person may know prayer requests from the church members, and everyone can agree together in the prayers for those needs. Someone else may carry an intercessory burden for a specific nation, and the whole group can pray together for it — even though they would have never prayed for those people in their personal prayer times.

Additionally, there seems to be some kind of unique power that God releases when His people gather. Here's what Jesus said:

> "Again I say to you that if two of you agree on earth concerning anything that they ask, it will be done for them by My Father in heaven. For where two or three are gathered together in My name, I am there in the midst of them." Matthew 18:19-20

The Bible has many similar verses about the power of agreement and unity.[15] When believers agree collectively regarding

---

15 Deuteronomy 32:30, Ecclesiastes 4:12, etc.

God's purposes, His kingdom is released into the earth in a distinctively powerful way.

What About the Secret Place?

You may find yourself uncomfortable with the idea that much of your prayer life should take place in community rather than privately. You may recall Jesus's teaching that when you pray, you should go to the secret place so no one sees what you are doing.

Jesus was not discouraging corporate prayer. I believe He was discouraging hypocritical and religious prayer. Let's review those verses.

> *"And when you pray, you must not be like the hypocrites. For they love to stand and pray in the synagogues and at the street corners, that they may be seen by others. Truly, I say to you, they have received their reward. But when you pray, go into your room and shut the door and pray to your Father who is in secret. And your Father who sees in secret will reward you. And when you pray, do not heap up empty phrases as the Gentiles do, for they think that they will be heard for their many words. Do not be like them, for your Father knows what you need before you ask him."*
> Matthew 6:5-8

The New Testament is full of examples and encouragements to participate in corporate prayer. Yet in this passage, it appears Jesus discouraged public prayer. Whenever you come to sections of Scripture that seem to contradict others, it is an invitation to deepen your understanding of God. There is always a revelation in the tension of Bible verses that are hard to reconcile. One of the simplest ways to reconcile them is to pay attention to their context.

Previously, I pointed out that Jesus, in the above passage, was not condemning repetition but "vain" repetition. Likewise, He was not condemning corporate prayer but self-focused prayer done to "be seen by others." He was not primarily concerned about *how* they were praying, but *why* they were praying in that way. When Jesus urged them to go away to a secret place to pray, He was reorienting them to intimacy with the Father, not discouraging corporate prayer.

You need both the secret place and the prayer meetings. You are to be a house of prayer individually and corporately. Your relationship with God is to be personal, but not private. Following Jesus is something you must do with others as the body of Christ. Corporate prayer must become prominent in the church again, as it was in the New Testament, so that we can be the house of prayer Jesus has called us to be.

If you are leading prayer meetings or would like to potentially start organizing prayer meetings, please check out the additional resources at enjoyingprayer.com.

UNCEASING: A MOVEMENT OF DAY AND NIGHT PRAYER

Last summer I had the privilege of visiting the small town of Herrnhut, Germany. I was invited to join a trip that coincided with the 300-year anniversary of the founding of their community. Despite a small population of less than 4,000 people, it boasts a miraculous legacy of affecting the world through prayer and missions. Count Ludwig von Zinzendorf founded Herrnhut when he provided the land as a place of refuge for protestant Christians who experienced persecution in the surrounding regions. Christians from various denominations flocked there to build a town from the ground up. The official anniversary of Herrnhut is the day that the first tree was felled to begin building homes for the refugees.

Eventually, many believers came together in the beautiful hills to worship. The Moravians established a small protestant church there. It was a hard and pioneering effort, but freedom was better than persecution. However, because these Christians were from such varied church traditions, they began to argue and divide over issues of Christian doctrine and practice. In response to the growing disputes, Zinzendorf began visiting the various homes in the community. He taught them from Scripture. He reminded them of the gospel and pleaded with them to forgive, reconcile, and unite around Jesus Christ. He was especially fascinated with the idea of Jesus as the humble Lamb of God. As the message of "the Lamb who was slain" spread through Herrnhut, God was preparing their hearts for an unexpected outpouring of the Holy Spirit that would reverberate into the nations of the earth.

August 13, 1727 became known as the Moravian Pentecost. As believers gathered for a communion service and reflected on the body and blood of Jesus, God moved powerfully. Brother and sisters confessed their sins, forgave each other, and were reconciled. Hearts began to heal and attitudes to change. Hunger for God grew.

Following this outpouring of the Spirit, they agreed to zealously seek the Lord in prayer. Forty-eight of these Moravians committed to establishing a 24/7 prayer watch together. Teams of two prayed for an hour each day — keeping every day covered in constant prayer. When they ran out of things to pray, they sang songs of praise and adoration to the Lamb. Interestingly, the word Herrnhut means "Watch of the Lord," and the Bible describes intercessors as watchmen..[1] A small community of only a few hundred believers continued this twenty-four-hour prayer schedule for over 100 years. From generation to generation, they continued to seek the Lord, worship Him with song, and intercede for the nations of the earth. Under the canopy of this incessant worship and prayer, God stirred the hearts of many of these Moravians to take the gospel to the hardest and darkest places around the world. A great missions movement was born out of their day-and-night prayer movement. Within a few decades, this one town had launched more missionaries to the nations than all Europe had sent in the one hundred years before them. Prayer and worship always fuels missions, discipleship, and evangelism.

---

1   Isaiah 62:6-7

One of the best summaries of the Moravian story is the book *Moravian Miracle* by Jason Hubbard. He says:

> What compelled them to pray around the throne, around the clock, and around the globe, and then to be sent on Gospel mission, was the worth of Jesus. Their purpose and mandate was to win for the Lamb who was slain the due reward of His suffering.[2]

The Spirit of the Moravians

During my visit to Herrnhut I heard stories from historians who have studied the journals and records of this incredible Moravian movement. I heard from seasoned saints who have lived there, laboring their whole lives for Herrnhut to enter back into its destiny as a place of catalytic prayer and missions. In fact, we were honored to help lead a few hours of worship and prayer during a three month, 24/7 worship and prayer gathering that was hosted in honor of the 300th anniversary.

The Moravians were not the first to organize 24/7 prayer in Christian history. During the Middle Ages, a number of monasteries kept vigils of unceasing prayer and worship; but the Moravian movement brought the idea of day-and-night prayer to the Protestant church. They also awakened a Protestant missions movement that prepared the way for William Carey, John Wesley, and others to lead great revivals in the coming years.

The Moravian zeal for prayer, revival, and missions is rising again — both in Herrnhut and around the world. During the Jesus People movement of the 1970s, the fire that visited the west coast of the United States spread all the way to Germany. A group of young believers in Herrnhut began to experience a move of God in their youth group. Eventually, they established

---

[2] *Moravian Miracle*, 2002, Pg 8

what is now called the Jesus Haus ("Jesus House"), a church and house of prayer committed to the original values of those early Moravian settlers and missionaries.

One evening during a service while I was there, Maren Winter, one of the founders of the Jesus Haus, recounted a story of James Goll visiting Herrnhut in the early 1990s. He prophesied of 120 houses of non-stop prayer around the world that would carry the "spirit of the Moravians."[3] Within a few years, the house of prayer movement as we know it was born and spread like wildfire around the world. More on that in a moment.

Maren also shared with us that at the Jesus Haus, they were installing an old bell tower from Herrnhut that had nearly been lost in a fire. It was installed and dedicated in July 2022. She prophesied to us that God used Herrnhut to inspire houses of prayer over the previous twenty years, but that His intention was not just to inspire houses of prayer; in the next season, she said God was going to "ring the bell" to awaken His church. I believe God desires the spirit of the Moravians to permeate the entire body of Christ as we are awakened to the reality of Jesus. The same values carried by the Moravians will fill the global church — day-and-night prayer, humility, brotherly love, beholding the Lamb of God, and a radical zeal for missions.

A Global 24/7 Prayer Movement

For the last twenty-plus years, there has been an unprecedented prayer movement across the earth. This movement has had many expressions, but one notable facet has been the phenomenon of 24/7 or day-and-night prayer. Experts who have studied the modern day prayer movement estimate that there were a few dozen groups organizing 24-hour prayer chains in the 1980s. By the early 2010s, there were an estimated 20,000 groups organized

---

[3] You can read about this in Goll's book *The Lost Art of Intercession*

UNCEASING: A MOVEMENT OF DAY & NIGHT PRAYER 161

to pray around the clock. This has never happened before. There are a few stories of perpetual prayer and worship throughout church history, such as the Moravians. But we have never seen a groundswell of 24/7 prayer across the earth as is happening right now in our lifetimes. The following paragraphs give some examples.

A few weeks ago I visited David's Tent DC, a tent of twenty-four-hour worship and prayer on the National Mall in Washington DC that began September 2015. Staffed by YWAM missionaries, David's Tent invites worship teams from across America to come throughout the year to help lead worship sets and enthrone Jesus at the United States capital.[4]

A few weeks before that I was at Gatecity Church in Atlanta, where they have been hosting twenty-four-hour prayer with live music since 2006.[5]

Last year I visited the International House of Prayer in Kansas City, which has been doing the same thing since 1999 — live worship music, ministry to the Lord, and intercessory prayer that never stops.[6]

During the pandemic of 2020, a few friends of mine launched the Global Family 24/7 virtual prayer room on Zoom with intercessors from around the world in an online, day-and-night prayer chain.[7]

Since 2017 Awaken the Dawn has hosted over 800 tent events that all included at least twenty-four hours of non-stop worship and prayer in public places.[8]

---

4 davidstentdc.org
5 gatecityatl.com
6 ihopkc.org
7 globalfamily24-7prayer.org
8 awakenthedawn.com

THIRTEEN

The 24-7 Prayer ministry based in the UK has logged over 22,000 prayer rooms—usually one week of day-and-night prayer—totaling over 500,000 hours of prayer. They launched in 1999.[9]

This is just a sampling of the day-and-night prayer that emerged in the early part of the twenty-first century. My examples are all based in the western world, but much of the 24/7 prayer movement is happening in Asia, Africa, and South America. It is springing up in a grassroots way and is impossible to track. The "spirit" of the Moravians is alive and well today![10]

As you continue your personal journey into an enjoyable life of prayer, the revelation of a global prayer movement should inspire you with strength and courage. You are not only trying to improve your personal spirituality; you are joining a sovereign move of God's Spirit that is swelling across the earth. Each of our individual prayers are part of a chorus of cries arising together to the throne of God. Just as Malachi prophesied, we are beginning to see incense arise in "every place" of the world.

> *For from the rising of the sun to its setting my name will be great among the nations, and <u>in every place incense will be offered to my name</u>, and a pure offering. For my name will be great among the nations, says the Lord of hosts.*
> *Malachi 1:11*

After years of observing what is happening around the world with day-and-night prayer, I believe that Scripture validates this historic movement.[11] The passages below not only give me

---

9   24-7prayer.com/about/about-us/who-we-are/
10   I share more about the 24/7 worship & prayer prayer movement in chapter six of my book *David's Tabernacle*.
11   It's worth noting that in the Bible, "day and night" does not always mean literally 24/7. Sometimes it does clearly, such as the heavenly throne room. Other times it could be "constantly" in a more loose sense. Either way, when something is happening "day and night," there's always the connotation of perpetual, unceasing activity.

biblical understanding for what God is doing, but they alert me to the importance of its timing. Many of the passages related to day-and-night prayer are also tied to the return of Jesus. Could a global day-and-night prayer movement be a sign of the times?

Biblical Example 1: The Heavenly Throne Room

The most obvious example of perpetual worship and prayer is the heavenly throne room. Jesus taught us to pray for heaven to come to the earth, and Revelation 4-5 gives us one of the clearest visions of what is happening in heaven. The angels and heavenly beings surrounding the throne of God are offering incessant songs of worship to the Lord.

> *And the four living creatures, each of them with six wings, are full of eyes all around and within, and <u>day and night</u> they never cease to say, "Holy, holy, holy, is the Lord God Almighty, who was and is and is to come!" Revelation 4:8*

These songs are mingled with the prayers and intercession of God's saints. Revelation 5:8 says that each of the twenty-four elders around the throne hold "a harp, and golden bowls full of incense, which are the prayers of the saints." These prayers and songs never end. There is day-and-night musical prayer and worship surrounding God in heaven right now. And one of the ways we can see God's kingdom increase on the earth is by doing on earth what they are already doing in heaven.

Biblical Example 2: David's Tabernacle

King David followed the heavenly pattern when he established his tent of worship in Jerusalem. The musical, prophetic, biblical, prayerful, intimate, day-and-night worship at David's tabernacle was heavenly worship. I talk much more about this in my book *David's Tabernacle*, but for this chapter I want to emphasize the fact that David's tabernacle was happening day and night. Here is the description of Levitical musicians and singers who ministered to God at the tent of David:

> Now these, the singers, the heads of fathers' houses of the Levites, were in the chambers of the temple free from other service, for they were on duty <u>day and night</u>.
> I Chronicles 9:33

David's tabernacle is the only Old Testament tabernacle that God has promised to restore again in the New Covenant[12]. While the restoration of David's tabernacle is a complex topic (I wrote an entire book on it), part of the restoration definitely includes the re-establishment of Davidic worship in the church.

As a global, singing, day-and-night prayer movement explodes around the world, we can easily connect the dots. Call it the spirit of the tabernacle of David. Call it the spirit of the Moravians. Call it a global prayer movement. Regardless of semantics, God is doing what He has promised to do!

Biblical Example 3: The Prophetess Anna

I have referenced the prophetess Anna several times in this book already, but I want to mention her once more in the context of this chapter. Here is how Luke describes her life of prayer and fasting:

> She did not depart from the temple, worshiping with fasting and prayer <u>night and day</u>. Luke 2:37b

As an individual, Anna could not have prayed 24/7 by herself. However, her prayer life was so radical and extravagant that she was described as worshiping, praying, and fasting "night and day." In other words, she was always at the Temple ministering to the Lord.

---

[12] Amos 9:11, Acts 15:16-17

I believe Anna is a type of the end-time church. Just as Anna partnered with God's promises through prayer to "birth" the first coming of Christ, the church at the end of the age will partner with the Spirit of God to "birth" the second coming of Christ through day-and-night prayer, intercession, and fasting. Could the day-and-night prayer movement that is emerging in our day be a collective "Anna" that is arising on the earth to precede the return of Jesus?

Biblical Example 4: The Persistent Widow

Jesus himself taught a parable about day-and-night prayer in Luke 18. We have previously discussed the main point of this parable as it relates to persistence in prayer. But note Jesus's language as he describes those who are persistent in faithful prayer:

> *And will not God give justice to his elect, who cry to him <u>day and night</u>? Will he delay long over them? I tell you, he will give justice to them speedily. Nevertheless, when the Son of Man comes, will he find faith on earth?" Luke 18:7-8*

I think Jesus is pointing back to the prophetess Anna here. Just as she ministered in the Temple night and day, those who pray persistently also cry out "day and night." Jesus was envisioning a people like Anna who pray continually, full of faith, confident in their identity in Him.

These few verses highlight the end-times context for the day-and-night prayer that Jesus describes. Jesus was prophesying the condition of the church when He comes again. When the Bridegroom returns, the Bride will be locked into day-and-night intimacy and intercession.

Is the current prayer movement the *final* swell of day-and-night prayer before Jesus comes again? That is yet to be seen. But it is certainly more than we have ever seen, and it should cause us to be sober-minded and alert.

Biblical Example 5: Watchmen on the Wall

Jesus's parable in Luke 18 stated clearly what Isaiah 62 prophesied many years earlier:

> On your walls, O Jerusalem, I have set watchmen; <u>all the day and all the night</u> they shall never be silent. Isaiah 62:6

In this passage, God has promised to raise up day-and-night praying communities around the world preceding Jesus's return[13]. The end-times watchmen never stop crying out to God. It is evident that God is the One who "sets" these watchmen into place. It is a sovereign work of the Lord, much like the modern prayer movement. This beautiful passage gives us another clear biblical promise that God wants to establish His people in continual prayer.

Closing Thoughts

How should you respond to this biblical call to day-and-night prayer? It is God who sets watchmen on the wall. The fact that you have read to the end of this book is an indicator that God is "setting" you on the wall of prayer— both in your personal prayer life and in a praying community. For some of you, this exploration into deep and enjoyable prayer has been brand new. You've learned many new concepts and ideas, and they are a launch point of faith into joyful and persistent prayer.

---

[13] Jesus's return is described with the language of God establishing Jerusalem as a "praise in the earth" in Isaiah 62:7

Others have become distracted, discouraged, and disconnected from God's heart in prayer. This book is an invitation for you to sign up again.

As you make decisions about how to implement the truths of this book in your daily life, remember you can't do it alone. When the apostle Paul says to "pray without ceasing,"[14] he is instructing the church, not just you or me as individuals. I cannot do this. You cannot do this. But God can do this. God *will* do this. And we can do it together as God's people, in partnership with Him, by His grace and the power of the Holy Spirit.

Remember that it all begins and ends with loving Him. True intimacy with God will always give birth to faithful intercession and bold mission that transform the world around us. Healthy intercessory prayer always flows from worshipful intimacy with the Lord. When you partner *with* the Lord, rather than just doing things *for* the Lord, you can experience fullness of joy because His presence is with you.[15] When prayer is about knowing and enjoying Jesus, you can find joy in His house of prayer.

May your journey of intimacy and intercession be filled with the joy of His nearness.

May you be filled with knowledge of God so that you know the One to whom you pray.

May you be rooted in your identity so that you know who you are to God as you approach Him.

May you experience the power of praise, intercession, petition, confession, and spiritual warfare.

May you have grace to prioritize God's presence in your life and in your schedule as you sing your prayers and pray the Scripture.

---

14 1 Thessalonians 5:17
15 Psalm 16:11

May prayer be a dialogue where you commune with God through His Word and Spirit.

May you experience the deep intimacy of travailing in intercession.

May you pray in the Spirit and with understanding.

May you be set in a community of praying believers who cry out together.

May day-and-night worship and prayer flood the nations of the earth.

May the church faithfully fast and pray until Jesus comes again.

And may we enjoy prayer because we enjoy Jesus!

Amen.

Please visit enjoyingprayer.com *for more practical resources on growing your prayer life—including content that did not make it into the book, podcasts, videos and more!*

ABOUT THE AUTHOR

FOR OVER TWENTY YEARS, Matthew Lilley has helped connect, equip and plant houses of prayer, praying churches and presence-centered communities. He is an author, worship leader, podcast host, and Bible teacher with a passion for God's presence, extravagant worship, and intercessory prayer. He founded Presence Pioneers in 2004 with a mission to build day and night worship and prayer for revival that touches the nations with the gospel of Jesus Christ. He is based at Opendoor Church in eastern North Carolina with his wife Shepard and their four children.

Visit Matthew's blog and website at **presencepioneer.com**.

BIBLIOGRAPHY

Bickle, Mike. *Growing in Prayer.* Lake Mary, FL: Charisma Media, 2014.

Bradshaw, David. *Awaken the Dawn.* Lake Mary, FL: Charisma House, 2021.

Duvall, J. Scott and Hays, Daniel. *God's Relational Presence.* Grand Rapids, MI: Baker Academic, 2019.

Engle, Lou. *Nazirite DNA.* Pasadena, CA: TheCall, Inc., 2010.

Greig, Pete. *God On Mute.* Ventura, CA: Regal Books, 2007.

Hubbard, Jason. *Moravian Miracle.* Unanderra NSW: Australian Heart Publishing, 2022.

Lewis, C.S. *The Weight of Glory.* New York, NY: HarperCollins Publishers, 1949.

Nouwen, Henri. *The Way of the Heart.* New York, NY: The Random House Publishing Group, 1981.

Prince, Derek. *Shaping History Through Prayer and Fasting.* New Kensington, PA: Whitaker House, 1973.

Tozer, A. W. *The Knowledge of the Holy.* New York, NY: HarperCollings Publishers, 1961.

———. *The Pursuit of God.* Harrisburg, PA: Christian Publications, Inc., 1948.

———. *Tozer on Christian Leadership.* Camp Hill, PA: Wingspread Publishers, 2001.

Virkler, Mark & Patti. *Four Keys to Hearing God's Voice.* Shippensburg, PA: Destiny Image Publishers, 2010.

PRESENCE PIONEERS MEDIA

Check out these other titles by Presence Pioneers Media

10 DAYS
by Jonathan Friz

DAVID'S TABERNACLE
by Matthew Lilley

Available wherever you buys books or at
presencepioneers.org

To get updates and discounts on future book releases visit
media.presencepioneers.org or scan the QR code below

www.ingramcontent.com/pod-product-compliance
Lightning Source LLC
Chambersburg PA
CBHW030328100526
44592CB00010B/608